SUSTAINABLE

DISRUPTION

Green Innovation Strategies That Generate Massive Returns

Oluwatosin Ajenifuja

Oluwatosin Ajenifuja

Sustainable Disruption: Green Innovation Strategies That Generate Massive Returns

Copyright © 2020

Published by:

Prodigy Press

www.prodigypress@gmail.com

CONTENTS

Preface iv

Foreword vi

Introduction viii

Chapter One: The Evolution of Disruption and the Rise of Sustainability 1

Chapter Two: The Economic Case for Green Innovation 8

Chapter Three: The Economics of Green Transformation 23

Chapter Four: The Economics of Green Capital and Sustainable Investment 39

Chapter Five: From Local Success to Global Sustainability Transformation .. 51

Chapter Six: Technology, Policy, and Culture in Sustainable Disruption 58

Chapter Seven: Redefining Value and Measuring Success in Green Innovation 65

Chapter Eight: Green Technology as the Core of Competitive Advantage 73

Chapter Nine: Policy, Regulation, and the Architecture of Sustainable Markets 81

Chapter Ten: Measuring Impact and Sustaining Growth in Green Innovation 89

PREFACE

The world stands at a defining crossroad where the old structures of profit maximization without responsibility colliding with the urgent demand for sustainability. The environmental crises that surround us are not abstract events happening in isolated parts of the world but deeply interconnected signals that call for an entirely new way of doing business. This book is not written as a manifesto of distant ideals but as a guide that demonstrates with clarity and precision how the next frontier of wealth creation will not come from extraction but from regeneration. Sustainable disruption is the language of this new era, and it speaks to those who understand that disruption alone is no longer sufficient. Innovation that destroys ecosystems or disregards future generations cannot be celebrated as progress because it creates a false economy built on depletion. Real progress is now defined by the balance between profitability and environmental intelligence, by the ability to achieve scale without devastation, and by the courage to redesign industries so that the planet becomes a stakeholder in every decision. This is not an easy journey, and it requires more than slogans about being green. It demands a rethinking of how capital is allocated, how supply chains are structured, how consumers are engaged, and how leaders embrace accountability as a source of strength rather than a burden. Throughout my years of research and observation of global markets, I have encountered a pattern that is impossible to ignore. Companies that invest early in sustainable practices do not just avoid regulatory penalties or protect their public image. They also outperform competitors financially in the long term, attract loyal customers who associate them with integrity, and secure partnerships that unlock new growth. Sustainability when applied strategically becomes a multiplier of returns rather than a cost. The old notion that being green is expensive and being profitable is incompatible with environmental responsibility is collapsing in front of us. In fact, the most disruptive companies of the future will not be those who simply digitalize processes or scale faster than competitors. They will be those who make sustainability the core of their disruption strategy, ensuring that every act of innovation leaves behind not scars but solutions. This book is designed for entrepreneurs, investors, executives, and policymakers who want to understand not just the why but also the how of sustainable disruption. Each chapter explores in depth the mechanisms through which businesses can innovate responsibly, build resilient models, and capture massive returns without compromising the ecological and social systems that support them. The lessons contained here are drawn from case studies across industries, from renewable energy to circular manufacturing, from ethical finance to green consumer goods. Together, they form a blueprint for anyone determined to thrive in the new economic order. I chose to write this book in a style that avoids unnecessary complexity because clarity is as important as depth in a subject that must be embraced by both experts and those just beginning their journey into sustainability. My intention is not to preach but to illuminate, not to demand blind compliance but to show the advantages of making sustainability inseparable from strategy. As you move through these pages, you will notice that sustainability is never framed as charity. It is positioned as strategy, a driver of innovation, and a powerful lens through which disruption finds lasting meaning. The central thesis is simple but powerful: sustainable disruption is not a compromise between doing well and doing good. It is the highest form of intelligent business, the meeting point where ethical leadership converges with unmatched profitability. This is not the future. This is the present, and the companies who see it first will be the ones who define the century ahead.

FOREWORD

Every generation inherits a set of challenges that forces it to reconsider the definition of progress. For the industrial age, progress was measured by the ability to mass produce. For the digital age, it was measured by the speed of connectivity. Today, our generation stands before a new challenge that cannot be ignored: how do we sustain life itself while still advancing economically. This question is not philosophical. It is deeply practical, for without a habitable planet no innovation, no technology, and no wealth accumulation will matter. What the author of this book has done is create not just an argument but a roadmap that proves sustainability and profitability are not enemies but allies when approached with foresight. As I read through these chapters, I was struck by the precision with which the author demonstrates how businesses across industries are already proving that sustainability can drive massive returns. These are not speculative theories but examples of transformation where renewable energy companies are outperforming fossil fuel incumbents, where circular economy startups are creating entirely new categories of value, and where consumers are rewarding transparency with loyalty. What impressed me most was the insistence that disruption on its own is insufficient. We have witnessed disruptive companies in technology, transport, and finance that changed markets but left behind negative externalities that we are still struggling to regulate. True disruption must now be measured not just by its ability to capture market share but by its ability to regenerate the systems on which it depends. In this regard, sustainable disruption is the highest level of innovation because it challenges entrepreneurs to consider the long horizon of their decisions and to design systems that endure beyond quarterly profits. The significance of this book lies in its refusal to frame sustainability as a burden. Instead, it elevates it to a competitive advantage, showing leaders that resilience, adaptability, and profitability all increase when businesses align with environmental and social responsibility. This is the kind of thinking that global markets desperately need at a time when climate change, resource scarcity, and shifting consumer values are reshaping what success looks like. As you read this book, prepare to encounter ideas that will stretch your imagination about what is possible. You will see that sustainability is not a cost center but a growth engine, not a trend but a transformation, and not a corporate obligation but a strategic weapon. The world has waited long enough for businesses to take responsibility, and those who act now will not only gain market leadership but also leave behind legacies that transcend financial metrics. It is my belief that this book will serve as a defining guide for leaders who refuse to accept the false choice between making money and making impact. If you are ready to embrace the reality that the future belongs to those who innovate sustainably, then this is the book you must read and the vision you must adopt.

INTRODUCTION

Every great economic transformation begins with a new way of seeing the world. The agricultural revolution was born from the realization that human societies could cultivate rather than chase sustenance. The industrial revolution was born from the recognition that machines could scale human productivity. The digital revolution was born from the discovery that information could travel instantly across the globe. Today we stand at the beginning of another revolution, one that redefines the very foundation of growth. It is the sustainability revolution, and its fuel is disruption. The paradox of our time is that while we have achieved unprecedented prosperity, we have also pushed the planet to its limits. Rising global temperatures, collapsing ecosystems, polluted air and water, and widening social inequalities are no longer distant warnings but daily realities. These crises are not side effects of progress. They are the direct consequences of a model of growth that celebrated disruption without responsibility. For decades, businesses were rewarded for scaling faster, consuming more, and externalizing costs onto societies and ecosystems. That era is ending, not because regulators demand it, but because the economic model itself is unsustainable. Consumers are choosing differently, investors are allocating capital differently, and technologies are enabling alternatives that make extractive systems obsolete. To ignore this shift is to walk willingly into irrelevance. Yet within this crisis lies the greatest opportunity of our time. Sustainable disruption is not about rejecting capitalism. It is about evolving it into a form that can endure. It challenges leaders to ask not only what markets they can dominate but also what legacies they will leave. It recognizes that businesses do not exist in isolation but in ecosystems that include communities, environments, and future generations. A business model that destroys its ecosystem is not only unethical but irrational. By contrast, a model that regenerates its ecosystem builds resilience, earns trust, and creates wealth that lasts. In this book you will discover how sustainable disruption functions as both philosophy and strategy. It is philosophy because it demands a new mindset where profit and purpose are not seen as rivals. It is strategy because it provides tangible pathways through renewable energy, circular economy practices, ethical supply chains, and green finance to achieve competitive advantage. We will explore how leading companies are transforming industries by embedding sustainability into design, production, distribution, and engagement. We will uncover the methods by which innovators are turning environmental challenges into business opportunities. And we will confront the reality that those who cling to outdated extractive models will eventually collapse under the weight of their unsustainability. The goal of this introduction is to prepare you for the journey ahead. Expect not just theories but actionable insights that you can apply regardless of whether you are leading a global corporation, building a startup, investing capital, or shaping policy. Expect to see sustainability reframed not as charity or compliance but as a generator of returns. Expect to be challenged to think beyond the next quarter and toward the next generation. Above all, expect to realize that sustainable disruption is not optional. It is inevitable, and the question is not whether you will adopt it but whether you will lead it or be overtaken by those who do. This is the threshold we now stand upon, and the decision is yours. The story of modern business has always been shaped by cycles of disruption, yet each cycle has left behind consequences that were not fully understood at the time. The industrial era gave us factories, railroads, and global trade, but it also introduced pollution on a scale never before experienced. The digital age gave us connectivity, innovation, and speed, but it also fueled consumption patterns that are draining resources at unsustainable rates. Today, the cycle we face cannot be addressed with patchwork solutions or half measures. It requires a redefinition of disruption itself. Sustainable disruption is not about slowing growth but about redirecting it so that the very engines of wealth creation also become engines of regeneration. This concept is not idealism; it is necessity. When resources become scarce, when regulations tighten, when consumers demand transparency, and when supply chains collapse under environmental stress, the only businesses that will thrive are those built to adapt and regenerate. Sustainability is no longer a conversation confined to activists, scientists, or policymakers. It is now a financial imperative recognized by the world's largest investors, banks, and corporations. To think of sustainability as separate from profitability is to misunderstand the forces reshaping the global economy. Climate change alone represents trillions of dollars in potential losses, but it also represents trillions in new opportunities for those who innovate with foresight. Consider the energy transition. Fossil fuels once defined national economies, dictated geopolitical strategies, and determined the fate of corporations. Yet today renewable energy is not just an ethical alternative but an economic juggernaut. Solar and wind are cheaper than coal and gas in most regions. Electric vehicles are outpacing traditional manufacturers. Investors are moving away from oil stocks and into green infrastructure. These shifts are not moral gestures but hard-nosed calculations of return. In the same way, industries from fashion to construction are being restructured by the logic of circularity. Products designed to last, materials designed to be reused, and processes designed to minimize waste are no longer experimental but competitive. Companies that resist these models may save money in the short term, but they will bleed relevance in the long run. The customer of today is not passive. They research where their products come from, how they are made, and what values the company stands for. Trust has become a currency, and sustainability is at its core. To lead in this era is to understand that green innovation is not only about protecting the environment. It is about protecting the future of your business. It is about ensuring that when the inevitable disruptions of climate change, social demand, and regulatory pressure collide, your organization stands as a resilient player rather than a casualty. This book calls upon leaders to think expansively. It demands that we ask difficult questions: Can an industry dependent on resource depletion truly survive in a resource-constrained world. Can a company that treats sustainability as a public relations exercise compete against one that embeds it deeply into its operating model. Can leaders who chase short-term profits without long-term responsibility expect to leave behind anything other than decline. These questions may seem daunting, but they are the foundation of opportunity. Within the challenge of sustainable disruption lies a chance to create markets that not only produce wealth but also heal the systems on which wealth depends. For example, technology companies can design platforms that optimize energy efficiency across cities. Agricultural firms can adopt regenerative practices that restore soil while feeding millions. Financial institutions can reimagine capital allocation to reward businesses that build rather than destroy. These are not distant possibilities. They are unfolding now, and the winners of the future will be those who accelerate them. The introduction of this book is not a ceremonial beginning but a call to awaken. It is a reminder that the old ways of thinking are collapsing and that clinging to them will ensure irrelevance. Disruption must evolve. It must carry within it not just the force of innovation but the wisdom of responsibility. Sustainable disruption is not a compromise; it is a superior strategy because it transforms the limitations of the present into the opportunities of the future. If disruption has always been about rewriting rules, then this is the moment to write the rules anew. Those rules must say that value is measured not just by financial gain but by the durability of ecosystems, the trust of consumers, and the stability of societies. This is where disruption earns permanence. This is where leaders move from short-lived victories to legacies that endure. As you continue through this book, allow this expanded introduction to frame every insight that follows. See sustainability not as a side conversation but as the central story of innovation in our century. Understand that what you hold is more than a guide; it is a compass pointing to a future where profitability and responsibility converge. The journey begins here, with a choice: to disrupt unsustainably and fade into irrelevance, or to disrupt sustainably and secure prosperity that lasts for generations.

CHAPTER ONE

The Evolution of Disruption and the Rise of Sustainability

Disruption has long been the defining characteristic of transformative business. From the earliest merchants who shifted local markets by opening new trade routes to the industrialists who introduced mass production and altered the very structure of economies, disruption has always carried with it the power to unsettle, realign, and redefine. Yet disruption by itself is neutral. It is neither inherently good nor inherently destructive. Its value is measured by the outcomes it produces, by the systems it shapes, and by the lives it touches. For much of modern economic history, disruption has been equated with speed, efficiency, and the aggressive capturing of markets, but little thought was given to the collateral damage such disruption produced. The industrial revolution, for example, was a marvel of human ingenuity that gave us railroads, electricity, steel, and global supply chains. It also gave us soot-filled skies, rivers poisoned with chemicals, sprawling slums built around factories, and an unprecedented dependence on fossil fuels that continue to dominate energy systems centuries later. Disruption made a few rich beyond measure, created industries that shaped nations, and transformed the human experience, but it also built the foundation of ecological degradation that we now struggle to repair. The digital revolution brought its own form of disruption; one marked by speed and connectivity. The arrival of the internet, mobile technology, and advanced computing connected billions of people across the globe, unleashed new industries, and democratized information. Yet, once again, disruption carried hidden costs. Massive amounts of e-waste now choke landfills, data centers consume extraordinary amounts of electricity, and the very platforms that promised to connect humanity often exacerbate polarization, misinformation, and social anxiety. In both industrial and digital disruption, we see the dual nature of innovation. It gives while it takes, it builds while it breaks, and it advances while it destroys. The central question of our time is whether disruption must always exact this dual price, or whether disruption can be redefined to serve not just the few but the many, not just the present but the future. It is here that sustainability enters not as an afterthought or a supplement but as the new definition of disruption itself. Sustainability, at its core, is about continuity, about ensuring that the systems which support life, business, and community remain intact for generations to come. It is about recognizing that no profit is worth achieving if the conditions for future profit are destroyed in the process. To merge sustainability with disruption is to evolve disruption itself, to move it from a narrow pursuit of efficiency to a broad pursuit of resilience. This evolution is not optional. It is being forced upon us by climate change, by consumer demand, by regulatory frameworks, and by the sheer unsustainability of extractive models. What makes this evolution remarkable is that it does not kill profitability but enhances it. Green innovation strategies are proving that the very act of aligning business with sustainability can unlock massive returns, not by ignoring responsibility but by embracing it as a driver of value. Consider the rise of renewable energy.

Where once fossil fuels were seen as irreplaceable, renewable solutions are now cheaper, cleaner, and increasingly more reliable. Disruption in the energy sector has merged with sustainability, and the result is both a reduction in carbon emissions and the creation of trillion-dollar markets. Similarly, the fashion industry, once notorious for waste, pollution, and exploitation, is now witnessing a wave of sustainable disruptors who embrace circular models, ethical sourcing, and transparency. These companies are not just surviving but thriving, capturing market share from legacy players while commanding loyalty from consumers who are increasingly conscious of the environmental and social impact of their purchases. The rise of sustainability as the defining characteristic of disruption can be seen as the natural next stage in the story of business evolution. First came the pursuit of efficiency, then the pursuit of connectivity, and now the pursuit of responsibility. The future will not be shaped by companies that simply scale faster or digitize better. It will be shaped by those who redefine disruption to mean regeneration, resilience, and renewal. This book is rooted in the belief that sustainable disruption represents not only a moral imperative but also the most intelligent business strategy available to us. By reframing disruption in this way, we can chart a course for businesses, industries, and economies that create wealth without destruction, innovation without depletion, and growth without collapse.

Green Innovation as the New Competitive Edge

For decades, competitive advantage was framed around cost efficiency, speed to market, and access to capital. Businesses were evaluated based on how well they could outproduce, outprice, or outmaneuver their competitors. Yet in the twenty-first century, the basis of competitive advantage is undergoing a dramatic transformation. Green innovation, once seen as a niche concern of environmentally conscious firms, has emerged as the new frontier of competitiveness across industries. Companies that embrace sustainability not only differentiate themselves but also secure advantages that traditional players can no longer replicate. Green innovation is not simply about replacing one material with another or adopting a few environmentally friendly practices. It is about reimagining business models from the ground up so that sustainability is built into the DNA of operations, supply chains, and customer engagement. When a company achieves this level of integration, it not only reduces costs by minimizing waste and increasing efficiency but also gains a reputational advantage that translates into long-term customer loyalty. One of the clearest demonstrations of this is in the energy sector. Renewable energy companies have gone beyond competing on price to create entirely new ecosystems of value. They partner with governments to shape infrastructure, they attract investment capital at unprecedented rates, and they scale globally without the same political and environmental risks faced by fossil fuel giants. In this way, their green innovation has not only positioned them competitively but has also reshaped the structure of the industry. In consumer markets, companies like those pioneering plant-based foods or sustainable fashion have used green innovation to turn consumer consciousness into market share. By aligning products with the values of a generation that demands ethical choices, they gain not just customers but advocates who amplify their brand. Green innovation thus becomes a form of cultural capital, one that legacy companies struggle to imitate because it is not built on marketing but on authenticity. Beyond consumer-facing industries, green innovation is transforming supply chains, manufacturing, and finance. Companies that adopt circular models reduce dependency on volatile resource markets, thereby shielding themselves from global disruptions. Financial institutions that prioritize sustainable investments are now outperforming those that cling to outdated portfolios, proving that capital flows to responsibility. Even technology companies, often criticized for their environmental footprint, are finding competitive advantage in building energy-efficient systems, reducing emissions, and designing for longevity. What unites these examples is the recognition that sustainability is no longer peripheral. It is central to the battle for competitive relevance. Green innovation acts as both shield and sword. It shields businesses from risks such as regulatory penalties, resource scarcity, and reputational damage, while simultaneously serving as a sword to capture new markets, attract investment, and inspire loyalty. For the modern entrepreneur, executive, or investor, the choice is not whether to adopt green innovation but how quickly it can be embedded into every aspect of strategy. Those who delay risk irrelevance, while those who act decisively will capture advantages that are not easily eroded. The rise of green innovation as the new competitive edge marks the beginning of an era where sustainability is no longer an externality. It is the core driver of profitability and the defining feature of industry leadership.

The Economics of Sustainable Disruption

For too long, the conversation around sustainability was framed in terms of sacrifice. Businesses were told that adopting green practices would increase costs, reduce efficiency, and limit growth. This perception created resistance, with many leaders seeing sustainability as incompatible with profitability. Yet recent decades have proven this to be a false dichotomy. The economics of sustainable disruption show that when sustainability is integrated intelligently, it produces massive financial returns, often greater than those achieved through traditional extractive models. The first economic principle of sustainable disruption is efficiency. When businesses reduce waste, optimize energy use, and design products for longevity, they cut costs dramatically. Efficiency is no longer just about speed or scale but about extracting maximum value from minimum input. Sustainability, by emphasizing resource efficiency, naturally drives businesses toward leaner, more profitable models. The second principle is resilience. Companies that rely heavily on finite resources or fragile supply chains face existential risks in a volatile global economy. Sustainable disruptors mitigate these risks by diversifying energy sources, adopting circular models, and building local supply networks. This resilience translates directly into financial stability, which investors reward with confidence and capital. The third principle is market demand. Consumers are voting with their wallets in favor of sustainability. Studies consistently show that people are willing to pay a premium for products that align with their values, and this willingness creates a pricing advantage for sustainable businesses. Moreover, younger generations, who represent the future of consumption, are even more committed to these values, ensuring that demand for sustainable products and services will only grow. The fourth principle is regulatory alignment. Governments worldwide are tightening regulations on emissions, waste, and resource use. Companies that proactively adopt sustainable practices avoid costly penalties, while those who lag behind face fines, restrictions, and reputational damage. By aligning early with regulatory trends, sustainable disruptors gain a head start that creates lasting economic advantage. The final principle is capital attraction. Investors increasingly recognize that unsustainable businesses carry unacceptable risks. Funds are flowing into green bonds, sustainable infrastructure, and companies with strong environmental, social, and governance practices. This shift in capital markets is not temporary but structural. The flow of capital toward sustainability ensures that disruptors who innovate responsibly will be rewarded with investment, while those who resist will struggle for financing. Together, these principles demonstrate that sustainable disruption is not a moral compromise but an economic strategy. The companies that understand this are already reaping rewards, while those that cling to outdated assumptions of sustainability as cost continue to decline. The economics are clear: green innovation does not hinder profit. It multiplies it. The future of wealth creation lies in sustainable disruption, and those who embrace it today will define the markets of tomorrow.

CHAPTER TWO

The Economic Case for Green Innovation

The conversation about sustainability has too often been framed as a moral appeal or an environmental responsibility detached from business imperatives, yet in reality the most compelling case for green innovation lies in its economic logic. Companies that embrace sustainability are not simply responding to ethical demands, they are positioning themselves to capture new markets, improve efficiency, and generate higher returns than those clinging to outdated practices. To understand this, one must look at the way global markets are shifting in response to both consumer expectations and regulatory frameworks. Consumers are no longer passive buyers of goods and services; they are conscious decision makers who increasingly align their purchasing power with their values. A study of global consumer behavior reveals that more than seventy percent of millennials and Gen Z consumers prefer to buy from companies that demonstrate environmental responsibility. This is not a trend confined to niche markets but a mainstream transformation of demand. Brands that fail to align with this shift risk not only reputational damage but declining sales, while those who take leadership in sustainability can command premium pricing and strengthen loyalty. The economic case becomes even clearer when examining the operational benefits of green innovation. Efficiency is the lifeblood of profitability, and sustainable practices almost always lead to cost savings. Whether it is through reducing energy consumption, minimizing waste, or optimizing supply chains, companies that integrate sustainable systems are discovering that they can cut costs significantly while simultaneously boosting their environmental credentials. Consider the case of energy-intensive industries like manufacturing. Firms that invest in renewable energy sources or energy-efficient equipment not only reduce their carbon footprint but also lower their long-term operational expenses, shielding themselves from volatility in fossil fuel markets. Waste reduction offers another compelling example. By adopting circular economy models where materials are reused, repurposed, or recycled, companies not only reduce environmental harm but also reduce procurement costs for raw materials. This creates a closed-loop system where resources generate value multiple times rather than being discarded after a single use. From an investor's perspective, the appeal of sustainable disruption is unmistakable. Capital is flowing toward businesses that integrate environmental, social, and governance criteria into their operations. Large institutional investors such as BlackRock and Vanguard are channeling billions into green funds, and this momentum shows no signs of slowing. Companies that cannot demonstrate long-term sustainability are increasingly viewed as high-risk investments, while those that embed sustainability into their models enjoy not only access to capital but also favorable valuations. Investors recognize that climate change, regulatory pressure, and consumer demand are structural forces that will determine which businesses thrive and which collapse. Green innovation is thus not a luxury; it is a prerequisite for long-term survival and prosperity. Governments and regulators around the world are also reinforcing this shift. Policies promoting renewable energy, carbon pricing, and sustainable production are no longer peripheral, they are central to economic planning. The European Union's Green Deal, for instance, commits hundreds of billions of euros to green initiatives, while countries such as China and the United States are investing heavily in renewable energy infrastructure. Companies that align themselves with these policy trends can access subsidies, tax breaks, and government contracts, while those that resist face fines, restrictions, and reputational damage. The regulatory landscape is becoming an accelerant of green innovation, ensuring that those who move first gain the largest advantage. The economic benefits also extend to talent acquisition and retention. Employees today, especially younger professionals, want to work for companies that align with their values. A company that demonstrates a genuine commitment to sustainability attracts top talent and reduces turnover, which in turn enhances productivity and creativity. In highly competitive industries where innovation is the key differentiator, the ability to attract and retain forward-thinking individuals can determine the difference between growth and stagnation. The story of Tesla offers a vivid case study of the economic case for green innovation. While traditional automakers hesitated to commit fully to electric vehicles, Tesla built its identity around sustainability and innovation. The result is not only leadership in the EV market but also a valuation that eclipses many of its competitors combined. This outcome was not the result of environmental advocacy alone but of recognizing that the future of mobility was inseparable from sustainability. By investing early and boldly in green technology, Tesla secured a dominant position in a rapidly expanding market. A similar dynamic is unfolding in industries ranging from fashion to agriculture. Sustainable fashion brands that emphasize recycled materials, ethical labor practices, and circular production are growing rapidly while traditional fast fashion brands face backlash for their environmental damage. In agriculture, companies that embrace regenerative farming practices are commanding higher prices and stronger relationships with retailers and consumers, while industrial agriculture faces criticism for its environmental degradation. Across every industry, the economic evidence is converging on a single truth: sustainability and profitability are not in conflict but in harmony. Furthermore, technological innovation is accelerating this convergence. Advances in artificial intelligence, blockchain, and data analytics are enabling businesses to monitor and optimize their sustainability practices with unprecedented precision. AI-powered systems can optimize energy usage in real time, blockchain can ensure supply chain transparency, and data analytics can identify inefficiencies that would otherwise go unnoticed. These technologies not only improve sustainability outcomes but also enhance operational performance, leading to stronger returns. In this sense, green innovation is not just about adopting environmentally friendly practices but about embracing a new technological paradigm that fuses efficiency with responsibility. Skeptics often argue that sustainability requires higher upfront investment, which is true in some cases, but this narrow focus on immediate costs ignores the broader financial picture. Investments in renewable energy, sustainable infrastructure, efficient technologies often pay for themselves many times over through reduced operating expenses, regulatory incentives, and enhanced consumer demand. The companies that hesitate are often those that suffer from short-term thinking, prioritizing quarterly profits over long-term value creation. Yet history shows that the firms willing to invest in transformative innovation are the ones that shape markets and dominate them. The economic case for green innovation is therefore inseparable from the concept of resilience. Businesses today face unprecedented levels of uncertainty from climate events, geopolitical instability, and supply chain disruptions. Companies that build sustainability into their core strategies are inherently more resilient because they rely less on volatile resource markets, are less vulnerable to regulatory shifts, and enjoy greater trust from both consumers and investors. Resilience is no longer an optional advantage, it is a survival strategy, and green innovation is its foundation. As we examine the trajectory of global markets, it becomes increasingly clear that the companies unwilling to embrace sustainable disruption will not only miss out on opportunities but risk obsolescence. The world is entering a new era where capital, talent, technology, and policy are all converging around sustainability as the defining principle of growth. Businesses that recognize this early and act decisively will not only generate massive returns but also shape the very future of commerce. Those who resist will fade into irrelevance, remembered not for their profits but for their inability to adapt. The economic case for green innovation is not about compromise; it is about clarity. It is about seeing the future not as a distant horizon but as a present reality unfolding before us. Every indicator, from consumer behavior to investor priorities, points to the same conclusion: sustainability is the most profitable path forward. Green innovation is not just an opportunity, it is the opportunity, and those who understand its economic power will define the next century of business.

Policy, Regulation, and the Global Green Economy

The global economic order has always been shaped by the architecture of policies and regulations that guide the flow of trade, capital, and innovation. In the nineteenth century governments drove the growth of railroads and industrial capacity, in the twentieth century they set the terms of globalization and financial liberalization, and in the twenty first century they are setting the framework for the green economy. The shift toward sustainability is not happening in isolation or as a spontaneous movement of individual corporations. It is being shaped, accelerated, and in some cases enforced by a rapidly expanding web of policies and regulations at national, regional, and international levels. For business leaders and entrepreneurs this regulatory transformation cannot be viewed as a constraint, it must be understood as a roadmap to future profitability. Those who align early with the emerging rules will position themselves at the forefront of new markets, while those who resist will find themselves penalized, excluded, or left behind. The European Union has taken the most aggressive and structured approach through the European Green Deal, which aims to make Europe the first climate neutral continent by 2050. This framework spans energy, industry, agriculture, and finance, introducing carbon pricing mechanisms, mandatory sustainability reporting, and incentives for renewable energy and circular economy models. For European companies these policies are not optional guidelines, they are binding requirements that are reshaping the way entire industries operate. A car manufacturer in Germany cannot ignore emissions standards without risking enormous fines, nor can an agricultural company in France ignore environmental regulations without losing subsidies. For non-European companies that want to access European markets, the rules are just as strict, meaning that the Green Deal extends its influence globally. This demonstrates how regulatory leadership in one region can reshape global supply chains. In the United States the regulatory environment has been less centralized but no less significant. Federal initiatives such as the Inflation Reduction Act have unleashed hundreds of billions in investments in clean energy, electric vehicles, and green infrastructure. State governments such as California have imposed their own strict environmental standards, setting de facto rules for entire industries. When California dictates emissions standards for vehicles, car manufacturers across the world must adapt because they cannot afford to lose such a large market. The United States is also leveraging financial incentives, tax credits, and procurement policies to stimulate green innovation. For businesses the lesson is clear: aligning with federal and state level sustainability goals is not just compliance, it is the key to accessing massive flows of public and private capital. China represents another dimension of the regulatory landscape. As the world's largest emitter of greenhouse gases, China faces enormous pressure to transition toward sustainability, yet it is also positioning itself as a leader in green industries. The Chinese government has invested heavily in solar manufacturing, electric vehicle production, and renewable energy infrastructure, creating a domestic regulatory environment that forces companies to adapt to sustainability goals while simultaneously creating export advantages. Chinese companies dominate global solar panel markets because of coordinated government policy, subsidies, and long term planning. This illustrates that policy is not merely about constraint but about industrial strategy. Countries that use regulation to guide industry toward sustainability are also seizing control of future markets. Beyond individual nations international agreements are playing a critical role. The Paris Agreement established a global framework for reducing emissions, creating momentum for national policies that enforce sustainability standards. While enforcement varies, the agreement has shaped expectations for businesses worldwide. Investors, insurers, and rating agencies now assess companies based on their alignment with the Paris targets, making international agreements economically relevant even when they are not legally binding. The regulatory landscape is also shifting in financial markets. Mandatory disclosure of environmental, social, and governance metrics is becoming common. The EU's Sustainable Finance Disclosure Regulation requires asset managers to report on the sustainability of their investments. The U.S. Securities and Exchange

Commission has proposed climate related disclosure requirements. These measures mean that companies cannot simply claim sustainability as a branding exercise, they must provide verifiable data. This transparency increases accountability and ensures that capital flows toward genuinely sustainable businesses. It also creates competitive advantages for firms that invest in robust reporting systems. Carbon pricing represents another powerful regulatory instrument. By putting a price on emissions governments create a direct economic incentive for companies to reduce their carbon footprint. The EU Emissions Trading System is the largest such mechanism in the world, but similar programs exist in countries from Canada to South Korea. For businesses carbon pricing is both a cost and an opportunity. Those that innovate to reduce emissions can save money and even profit by selling unused allowances, while those that fail to adapt face rising costs that erode competitiveness. Carbon pricing is not only a tool for emission reduction but also a driver of innovation, forcing companies to explore cleaner processes, products, and business models. Regulations are also reshaping supply chains. Laws requiring due diligence on environmental and social practices are becoming more common. The German Supply Chain Due Diligence Act requires companies to ensure that their suppliers comply with human rights and environmental standards. Similar measures are being introduced in other countries, meaning that businesses must examine not only their direct operations but their entire value chain. This creates complexity but also opportunities for innovation in supply chain management. Technologies such as blockchain are being deployed to ensure transparency, enabling companies to comply with regulations while building consumer trust. The rise of green finance is also intertwined with regulation. Central banks and financial regulators are increasingly requiring financial institutions to assess climate related risks. This shifts capital away from carbon intensive industries and toward sustainable ones. Green bonds, sustainability linked loans, and climate focused funds are expanding rapidly, supported by regulatory frameworks that standardize definitions and reporting. For businesses this means that access to capital is increasingly tied to sustainability performance. A company that fails to align with environmental goals will find it harder to raise money, while those that embrace green innovation will enjoy privileged access to funding. For entrepreneurs' policy and regulation must be seen as signals rather than obstacles. Regulations indicate where markets are moving and where capital will flow. A startup that anticipates upcoming rules can position itself ahead of competitors. For instance a company developing energy storage solutions is not simply addressing current demand but is preparing for a regulatory environment where renewable energy integration is mandatory. Similarly businesses that invest in sustainable packaging are preparing for regulations banning single use plastics. Regulation is often seen as reactive, but for the astute entrepreneur it is predictive, pointing toward inevitable transformations in markets. Importantly the regulatory landscape is not uniform across the world, which creates both challenges and opportunities. Companies operating in multiple jurisdictions must navigate a patchwork of rules, but they can also exploit leadership in one region to set global standards. A firm that develops technology to comply with European sustainability requirements can market itself globally as a leader in compliance and innovation. In this sense strict regulations can become a competitive advantage. Businesses that learn to innovate under pressure can outcompete those in less regulated environments when global standards converge. The intersection of policy, regulation, and the green economy is also shaping consumer perception. Governments and international bodies are not only enforcing sustainability through law, but they are also educating the public and shaping expectations. Campaigns to reduce plastic use, encourage recycling, or promote renewable energy shift consumer attitudes in ways that reinforce regulatory goals. This creates a feedback loop where regulation influences behavior and behavior creates political support for more regulation. Businesses that ignore this loop will find themselves out of step not only with the law but also with their customers. The regulatory wave is only beginning. As climate impacts intensify and social movements demand accountability, governments will impose stricter rules, higher penalties, and more ambitious targets. Companies that resist will find themselves in constant conflict, incurring costs and losing goodwill. Those that embrace regulation as a guide to innovation will thrive in the green economy. History shows that disruptive innovation often emerges in response to regulation. Safety standards gave rise to safer automobiles, financial regulation created stronger banking systems, and environmental regulation will now give rise to more resilient and profitable businesses. The conclusion is unavoidable: regulation is not an external burden but an internal driver of transformation. Companies that integrate regulatory foresight into their strategy are not merely surviving; they are creating the conditions for leadership. The global green economy is being built by policies and laws that redefine what is possible, and only those who adapt quickly will capture its immense rewards.

Consumer Demand and Market Transformation

No force has reshaped modern markets as dramatically as the collective power of consumers who today act not merely as passive buyers but as active participants in shaping the values and directions of industries. The rise of conscious consumerism has created a reality where sustainability is no longer an optional gesture but a prerequisite for relevance. Businesses that fail to meet this rising tide of demand for green innovation risk not only declining sales but reputational collapse. Those that embrace it however are discovering that sustainability is not a sacrifice but a source of differentiation, loyalty, and growth. The psychology of the modern consumer reveals why this transformation is so powerful. In earlier decades most purchasing decisions were driven by price and convenience, but in today's hyper connected world consumers are equipped with information at their fingertips. They can instantly research where a product was sourced, how it was manufactured, and whether the company behind it operates responsibly. Social media amplifies both praise and criticism, rewarding companies that align with consumer values and punishing those that violate them. A single viral post exposing environmental harm can devastate a brand, while a campaign highlighting authentic sustainability efforts can spark unprecedented growth. This shift is not limited to niche markets of environmentally conscious buyers; it extends across demographics and geographies. Surveys consistently show that millennials and Gen Z, who now represent the fastest growing consumer groups, overwhelmingly prefer brands that prioritize sustainability. Even baby boomers, often considered less value driven in purchasing, are increasingly adopting green preferences, especially in sectors like food, personal care, and energy. This multi-generational shift ensures that the demand for sustainable products is not a temporary fad but a structural transformation of the marketplace. Market transformation becomes even clearer when analyzing specific industries. In fashion the rapid rise of sustainable brands has forced traditional fast fashion companies to rethink their models. Shoppers are increasingly demanding transparency about sourcing, working conditions, and environmental impact. Brands that ignore these demands face backlash, while those that adopt circular economy practices, such as clothing recycling and resale platforms, are capturing market share. The resale fashion market alone has grown into a multibillion dollar industry, demonstrating that consumers are not only willing to buy sustainable products but eager to embrace new consumption models. In the food industry the rise of organic, plant based, and locally sourced products illustrates the same pattern. Consumers are shifting their diets to reduce environmental impact, creating booming demand for alternatives such as plant based proteins. Companies that anticipated this trend, like Beyond Meat and Impossible Foods, achieved explosive growth by aligning with consumer values, while traditional meat producers are scrambling to adapt. Even in mainstream grocery retail, sustainability has become a competitive differentiator, with major chains marketing their commitments to reducing plastic, sourcing responsibly, and supporting local farmers. The energy sector provides another striking example of market transformation. For decades energy was viewed as a commodity where price dictated choice, but today consumers are demanding renewable options even when they cost slightly more. Utilities offering green energy plans are experiencing increased customer retention, while rooftop solar adoption is skyrocketing as households seek to align their consumption with their values. The transformation is so profound that entire communities are forming around renewable energy cooperatives, demonstrating how consumer demand can drive systemic change. Transportation, too, has been reshaped by consumer expectations. The surge in demand for electric vehicles is not solely the result of regulation or subsidies; it is also the product of consumers demanding cleaner alternatives. Tesla's rise, for instance, was fueled not just by technological innovation but by consumers who wanted their cars to reflect their environmental values. As more automakers introduce electric models, consumers are rewarding those who combine sustainability with performance and design. The result is an irreversible shift where the market for internal combustion vehicles is shrinking and the market for electric vehicles is expanding at exponential rates. The hospitality and tourism sectors further illustrate the breadth of this transformation. Travelers are increasingly seeking ecofriendly hotels, carbon neutral flights, and sustainable experiences. Companies that integrate sustainability into their offerings not only attract these consumers but also command premium pricing. Luxury hospitality groups that once focused solely on exclusivity are now highlighting their commitments to conservation, renewable energy, and community support, because they recognize that consumer demand is shifting their industry's foundations. At the heart of consumer driven market transformation is trust. Consumers no longer take corporate claims at face value. They demand transparency, verification, and measurable impact. This is why certifications such as Fair Trade, Rainforest Alliance, and B Corp have become powerful market signals. They allow consumers to distinguish genuine commitments from greenwashing. For companies the implication is clear: sustainability cannot be a superficial branding exercise, it must be authentic, consistent, and demonstrable. Companies that attempt to manipulate or mislead consumers with hollow claims often face severe backlash when their practices are exposed. Authenticity is not a soft value; it is a market necessity. Digital platforms amplify the influence of consumers and accelerate market transformation. Online reviews, social media activism, and influencer partnerships shape consumer perceptions in real time. A single endorsement from a respected sustainability influencer can drive significant sales, while a coordinated boycott campaign can cripple a brand. The democratization of information has shifted power away from corporations and into the hands of consumers, making responsiveness to consumer values a core competitive requirement. One cannot underestimate the role of younger consumers in driving long term market change. Generation Z, the first generation to grow up entirely in a digitally connected world, is the most sustainability conscious demographic in history. Their expectations are shaping not only current markets but future ones. As they grow in purchasing power and enter positions of corporate influence, their preferences will become the dominant force shaping industries. Businesses that ignore this generational shift risk long term irrelevance. The implications of consumer driven transformation extend beyond individual industries to the structure of global trade. Companies seeking to access international markets must align with the sustainability preferences of consumers across regions. For instance Asian manufacturers exporting to Europe or North America must meet the sustainability standards demanded by consumers there, or they risk exclusion. In this way consumer preferences are shaping not only local markets but global supply chains, reinforcing the importance of green innovation as a universal business strategy. Importantly consumer demand does not only apply pressure, it creates opportunity. Companies that innovate to meet sustainability expectations can unlock entirely new markets. The rise of reusable packaging solutions, shared economy platforms, and carbon neutral services illustrates how consumer demand can drive the creation of new business models. Entrepreneurs who listen carefully to these signals are able to design products and services that not only meet demand but redefine industries. For example companies offering subscription based clothing rental services are thriving because they align with consumers who value sustainability without sacrificing choice or style. Financial markets are also responding to consumer demand, creating a cycle where consumer preferences influence investment flows. As consumers direct their spending toward sustainable products, investors direct their capital toward sustainable businesses. This reinforces market transformation by ensuring that companies aligned with sustainability enjoy both consumer loyalty and financial backing, while those that resist face declining revenue and shrinking access to capital. The convergence of consumer demand and investor priorities creates a powerful alignment that accelerates green innovation. It is important to acknowledge that consumer demand alone cannot solve systemic sustainability challenges, but it is a catalyst that pushes companies and governments to act more decisively. Policymakers respond to voter preferences, investors respond to market trends, and businesses respond to customer expectations. In this sense consumer demand is not merely shaping markets, it is reshaping the broader economic and political systems that govern sustainability. For businesses the conclusion is straightforward: consumer demand for sustainability is not a passing phase but a defining feature of the twenty first century economy. Companies must treat it as a central element of their strategy. Those who embrace it will gain not only sales but loyalty, resilience, and influence. Those who dismiss it will face erosion of trust, shrinking market share, and eventual irrelevance. The transformation of markets through consumer demand is relentless because it is anchored in values, and values once established are not easily reversed. The future of commerce belongs to those who recognize that every purchase is more than an exchange of money for goods, it is a statement of identity, values, and responsibility. When consumers choose sustainable products they are voting for a different kind of economy, one where profit and responsibility converge. Businesses that help enable this choice will thrive, while those that ignore it will be left behind. In conclusion consumer demand is not just shaping markets, it is transforming them at their core. The voice of the consumer has become the most powerful driver of green innovation, propelling industries into new models of production, distribution, and accountability. The companies that listen to this voice, that honor it with authenticity and foresight, will not only survive but define the future. Market transformation is not a possibility, it is already here, and it is the consumer who has written its rules.

CHAPTER THREE

The Economics of Green Transformation

T he conversation about sustainable disruption often begins with values and visions, but it ultimately rests on the foundation of economics. If sustainability cannot prove itself as economically viable, it risks being dismissed as philanthropy or symbolic rhetoric rather than an engine of transformation. The economics of green transformation therefore become the pivot on which the future of industries and nations will turn, because money drives markets, incentives shape behavior, and financial realities determine whether companies adopt green innovation as a strategic imperative or treat it as a short-term marketing tactic. The first economic truth of green transformation is that sustainability is no longer a cost center, it is a profit driver. Businesses once assumed that adopting environmentally responsible practices would mean increased expenditure with little or no return. For decades, the conversation was framed as a trade-off, where being green meant giving up profitability for responsibility. But a new reality is emerging where the firms that take sustainability seriously are outperforming competitors on growth, profitability, and long-term resilience. This is partly because consumers are voting with their wallets, but more importantly, it is because resource efficiency, energy optimization, waste minimization, and supply chain transparency lead to reduced costs and improved margins when implemented strategically. Consider energy. Traditional fossil-based operations have faced increasing volatility, price shocks, and regulatory scrutiny. Companies that invest in renewable energy infrastructures such as solar, wind, and geothermal are creating stable long-term cost savings that insulate them from energy market disruptions. The upfront costs are significant, but once installed, renewable systems drastically reduce operational expenses. This explains why global giants across manufacturing, technology, and retail are racing toward renewable energy adoption. In purely economic terms, energy is a predictable expense and lowering it means increasing profit margins without compromising output. This illustrates the underlying principle of green transformation economics: investing in sustainability is not about charity but about strategic resource control. Another critical dimension is supplying chain management. The global economy is tightly interconnected, and supply chains represent both risk and opportunity. Unsustainable supply chains tend to depend on resource extraction practices that invite regulatory penalties, reputational damage, and geopolitical risks. In contrast, supply chains that prioritize sustainable sourcing build resilience, strengthen supplier relationships, and unlock new customer markets that demand ethical practices. Economically, this translates into reduced volatility, more predictable costs, and an improved brand premium. When consumers are willing to pay more for ethically sourced products, the company creates both social value and economic gain. The relationship between regulation and profitability is another key factor. While businesses often resist regulatory pressures, forward-looking companies recognize that aligning ahead of regulation creates a first-mover advantage. Governments worldwide are tightening carbon reporting, waste management, and emissions policies. Those who innovate early to meet future standards will spend less than those forced to react at the last minute. Furthermore, early adopters are able to influence regulation itself, shaping industry norms in ways favorable to their own strategic positioning. Economically, this means that green innovators not only avoid penalties but also capture market leadership. Investors are also reshaping the economics of sustainability. The rise of ESG investing has moved trillions of dollars toward companies that demonstrate strong environmental, social, and governance performance. Access to capital is the lifeblood of any company, and businesses that prove themselves credible on sustainability metrics attract more investment at better rates. Conversely, companies that ignore sustainability face divestment, reduced valuations, and higher risk premiums. This creates a self-reinforcing cycle where the economics of capital allocation reward green innovation and punish environmental neglect. It is not philanthropy but financial pragmatism that is driving this transition. A deeper analysis reveals that the economics of green transformation extend beyond company-level profitability to macroeconomic competitiveness. Nations that lead in renewable energy, sustainable technologies, and green infrastructure will secure the industries of the future. Their workforces will acquire the skills demanded by global markets, their economies will generate exportable innovations, and their societies will benefit from improved health outcomes due to reduced pollution. Meanwhile, countries that cling to outdated carbon-heavy models risk falling behind in both competitiveness and attractiveness to global investors. The economic race for sustainability is therefore geopolitical in nature, with first-mover nations positioned to dominate future growth sectors. Within industries, the economic incentives of green transformation play out differently but with the same underlying logic. In manufacturing, resource efficiency reduces waste, lowers costs, and improves margins. In real estate, green buildings command higher rents and valuations while lowering operational expenses for tenants. In agriculture, sustainable practices preserve soil health and secure long-term yields. In transportation, electric and hybrid models are rapidly lowering lifetime ownership costs. Across all these sectors, the same pattern emerges sustainability creates new value streams while simultaneously protecting against risks, leading to superior economic outcomes. Critics often raise the question of scale, arguing that while small pilot projects may show positive returns, scaling sustainability across global operations can be prohibitively expensive. This critique overlooks the fact that technological innovation consistently reduces costs over time. Renewable energy, once prohibitively costly, is now cheaper than fossil fuel generation in many regions. Electric vehicle batteries have fallen dramatically in price. Circular economy business models that once seemed unrealistic are now producing profitable ventures. The economics of green transformation must be viewed dynamically, not statically. What is costly today will often be profitable tomorrow, and those who invest early reap the greatest long-term rewards. Another underappreciated economic element is talent. In a competitive global labor market, the best employees increasingly want to work for companies that align with their values. Businesses that lead in sustainability gain a talent advantage, attracting skilled professionals who drive innovation, productivity, and growth. Employee retention improves when workers feel they are contributing to meaningful goals. Turnover is expensive, recruitment is competitive, and productivity gains from motivated employees are significant. Thus the economics of sustainability extend into human capital advantages that reinforce financial performance. The transition to a green economy is not without risks, but these risks are manageable and outweighed by the opportunities. Transition costs can be high, requiring capital investments in new technologies and processes.

Market demand can fluctuate as consumer preferences evolve. Regulations can be uneven across regions, creating complexity. But when compared to the risks of inaction—rising energy costs, stranded assets, reputational damage, investor flight, and regulatory penalties—the economics clearly favor proactive transformation. Ultimately, the economics of green transformation rest on a simple principle: sustainability is no longer a moral choice but a market necessity. The businesses that understand this truth will thrive, while those that resist will decline. Markets reward efficiency, innovation, and risk management, all of which are inherent to green strategies. As technology advances and consumer demand accelerates, the gap between sustainable and unsustainable businesses will widen into a chasm. Those who stand on the wrong side will find themselves priced out of relevance, while those who embrace transformation will enjoy not just survival but dominance. For entrepreneurs, executives, policymakers, and investors, the economic case for green transformation is overwhelming. The question is not whether it will happen but how quickly one chooses to adapt. And in a world where markets move faster than ever, hesitation is the most expensive choice of all.

Long Term Value Creation Through Sustainability

The true measure of any business, nation, or movement is not its immediate success but its enduring impact. Short term profits can be impressive, rapid growth can be celebrated, but the legacies that stand the test of time are built on long term value creation. In the age of disruption, sustainability is emerging as the cornerstone of enduring value, not because it is fashionable but because it is indispensable to survival. The future belongs to the companies and societies that recognize sustainability not as a cost but as a growth engine that compounds value over decades. Understanding this requires us to distinguish between short term gains and long term value. Short term gains are often generated by cost cutting, market manipulation, or exploiting temporary advantages. They satisfy quarterly reports and investor impatience but do little to secure the foundation of future prosperity. Long term value, in contrast, comes from strategies that build resilience, trust, and relevance. It is the product of sustained investment in systems that adapt to change, preserve resources, and align with societal expectations. In this sense, sustainability is not only compatible with long term value creation, but also the very essence of it. One of the keyways sustainability that creates long term value is through risk mitigation. Every business faces risks from market volatility, regulatory change, technological disruption, and reputational damage. Unsustainable practices amplify these risks by exposing businesses to regulatory penalties, consumer backlash, and supply chain disruptions. Sustainable practices, on the other hand, reduce vulnerability by aligning with emerging regulations, meeting consumer demands for responsibility, and securing resilient supply chains. By reducing exposure to risks that can erode value, sustainability preserves and extends the lifespan of business advantage. Trust is another vital element of long term value creation, and it is impossible to build lasting trust without sustainable practices. Consumers are increasingly skeptical of companies that fail to demonstrate transparency and responsibility. They want to know not only what a product costs but also where it comes from, how it is made, and what impact it has on the environment and society. Businesses that provide these assurances build trust that translates into loyalty, advocacy, and premium pricing. Trust, once earned, compounds over time, creating brand equity that shields businesses against competitors and market fluctuations. Without sustainability, trust is fragile and easily lost, making it difficult for any organization to sustain long term value. Long term value is also driven by the ability to adapt to change, and sustainability equips businesses with this adaptability. The transition to a low carbon economy, the digitization of industries, the rise of conscious consumers, and the shifting priorities of investors all represent fundamental changes to the business landscape. Companies that embed sustainability into their strategies position themselves to adapt quickly, because they are already aligned with these macro trends. Their products, processes, and philosophies are built with resilience in mind, allowing them to pivot more effectively as external conditions evolve. This adaptability is itself a form of value creation, as it ensures that organizations remain relevant and competitive over time. Innovation, as discussed earlier, is critical to sustainable growth, but it also underpins long term value creation. Businesses that continuously innovate sustainable solutions position themselves not only as current leaders but as future shapers. By investing in research, development, and partnerships that push the boundaries of possibility, they build intellectual property, brand reputation, and market influence that extend their value far beyond immediate profits. Innovation compounds value by creating ecosystems of products and services that reinforce one another, ensuring that companies remain indispensable to their customers for years or decades. Human capital plays a crucial role in long term value creation, and sustainability has a profound impact on this dimension. Employees today want more than a paycheck; they want purpose, belonging, and the chance to make a difference. Companies that embrace sustainability attract and retain top talent who are motivated to contribute to meaningful goals. Over time, this leads to stronger organizational cultures, higher productivity, and deeper innovation pipelines. Employee engagement is not a soft metric but a driver of long term profitability, and sustainability is increasingly central to achieving it. An organization that invests in the wellbeing of its people, communities, and environment fosters loyalty and creativity that create enduring advantages. Another critical mechanism for long term value creation is capital allocation. Investors are increasingly rewarding companies with credible sustainability strategies because they represent lower risks and higher long term growth prospects. Funds that prioritize environmental, social, and governance criteria are directing capital toward businesses that align with sustainable practices. This influx of patient capital strengthens balance sheets, reduces cost of capital, and provides resources for continued innovation. Companies that fail to embrace sustainability, on the other hand, are seeing divestment, higher financing costs, and declining valuations. This divergence in investor behavior amplifies over time, ensuring that sustainable businesses continue to grow stronger while unsustainable ones weaken. Long term value also depends on a company's ability to maintain relevance in the eyes of society. Societal expectations evolve, and businesses that ignore them risk obsolescence. Issues such as diversity, inclusion, climate responsibility, and ethical sourcing are no longer peripheral but central to consumer decisions. Companies that proactively align with these expectations secure cultural relevance that enhances their legitimacy and influence. Over decades, this relevance builds an enduring place for the company in society, ensuring that it remains not only profitable but also respected. Cultural legitimacy is a form of intangible capital that compounds into long term value. Sustainability contributes to long term value at the macroeconomic level as well. Nations that prioritize sustainability secure advantages in competitiveness, innovation, and global leadership. Their industries are better prepared to export sustainable solutions, their workforces are skilled in emerging technologies, and their infrastructure is aligned with the demands of a low carbon economy. This national resilience attracts foreign investment; boosts trade and enhances geopolitical influence. For companies operating within these nations, the supportive ecosystem creates fertile ground for long term growth. Thus, sustainability at the national level reinforces sustainability at the corporate level, creating a virtuous cycle of value creation. A key insight into long term value creation is that sustainability transforms the concept of profit itself. Traditional models define profit narrowly as financial gain after expenses. Sustainable models expand profit to include social and environmental returns. This expanded definition reflects the reality that businesses do not operate in isolation but within societies and ecosystems. When companies generate social value through job creation, education, or community development, they build goodwill that sustains their license to operate. When they protect ecosystems and reduce environmental harm, they preserve the natural capital upon which all economic activity depends. These forms of value, though sometimes intangible in the short term, accumulate over time into enduring competitive advantage. Critically, long term value creation through sustainability requires a mindset shift among leaders. It demands moving from a quarterly mindset to a generational mindset, where decisions are evaluated not only for immediate impact but for their implication decades into the future. This does not mean ignoring short term performance but aligning it with long term goals. Companies must learn to communicate this alignment to investors, customers, and employees, demonstrating how sustainable strategies deliver both immediate returns and future resilience. Leaders who master this narrative build confidence among stakeholders that compounds into long term support and loyalty. One of the greatest obstacles to long term value creation is the persistence of short term thinking. Quarterly earnings pressures, shareholder demands, and competitive rivalries often push companies to prioritize immediate results over future prosperity. Overcoming this requires courage and clarity of vision. It also requires the ability to educate stakeholders about the economic logic of sustainability, showing that long term investments in renewable energy, circular models, and sustainable innovation will generate superior returns over time. Transparent reporting, clear milestones, and consistent delivery on promises to build the credibility necessary to maintain stakeholder patience. Case studies illustrate how long term value emerges from sustainable practices. Unilever, for example, has pursued a Sustainable Living Plan that integrates sustainability into every aspect of its operations. Over time, its sustainable brands have outperformed others in growth and profitability. Patagonia has built a global reputation and loyal customer base by embedding sustainability into its identity, leading to decades of growth and cultural influence. Tesla, by positioning itself as a sustainable innovator, has not only disrupted the automotive industry but also created immense shareholder value despite skepticism. These examples demonstrate that sustainability is not only compatible with long term value but the surest path to achieving it. Looking ahead, long term value creation will increasingly depend on sustainability because the external pressures are intensifying. Climate change impacts are becoming more visible, resource scarcity is tightening supply chains, and societal expectations are rising. Businesses that cling to short term exploitation will find themselves facing mounting costs, declining trust, and shrinking opportunities. Conversely, those that embrace sustainability will not only survive these pressures but transform them into platforms for growth. The compounding effect of sustainable practices means that the earlier they are adopted, the greater the long term returns. Leaders must therefore act with urgency, recognizing that hesitation reduces future value while decisive action multiplies it. Ultimately, long term value creation through sustainability is about building legacies. It is about ensuring that companies, industries, and societies contribute positively to the future rather than depleting it. It is about moving from exploitation to stewardship, from extraction to regeneration, and from short term thinking to generational vision. Businesses that succeed in this transformation will not only secure their profitability but also their relevance, influence, and impact for decades to come. Sustainability is not a trend or an obligation. It is the foundation of enduring prosperity. By embedding sustainability into every decision, every innovation, and every strategy, leaders create value that compounds across generations. This is the essence of sustainable disruption: not only to survive the present but to shape the future in ways that generate massive returns both financial and societal.

Green Transformation as a Competitive Edge in Global Markets

The transformation toward green innovation is no longer a marginal trend or a response to regulatory pressure, it has evolved into a defining force that shapes global markets and separates enduring leaders from lagging competitors. At the heart of this transformation lies the recognition that sustainability is not a charitable obligation but an economic advantage when strategically integrated into the very DNA of a business. Companies that understand this shift are not only future-proofing their operations but also seizing opportunities to redefine industries, expand into new markets, and cultivate loyal consumer bases that value responsibility as much as they value quality and affordability. When examined closely, it becomes evident that green transformation is not simply about operational changes or cost efficiencies but about creating a holistic ecosystem of value that resonates with stakeholders across borders. The competitive edge emerges from the ability to align purpose with profitability, resilience with growth, and innovation with long-term sustainability. The process requires commitment, foresight, and willingness to challenge established business models, but the rewards far exceed the risks. One of the primary drivers that make green transformation a source of competitive edge is the global shift in consumer expectations. Across regions and demographics, consumers are increasingly conscious of how the products they purchase are sourced, manufactured, packaged, and delivered. Younger generations in particular are vocal and intentional about their preference for brands that demonstrate ethical practices and environmental stewardship. This is not confined to luxury markets or niche sectors; it is a mass-market phenomenon. From food and beverages to technology and fashion, sustainability is influencing purchasing decisions in ways that shape entire industries. Brands that fail to respond risk being perceived as outdated or careless, while those that embrace transparency and green innovation position themselves as leaders who respect the values of their customers. The ability to translate sustainability into authentic storytelling and measurable action becomes a magnet for loyalty, allowing businesses to expand their share of wallet and attract premium pricing even in competitive markets. Another dimension of competitive advantage comes from efficiency gains and risk management. While many organizations still perceive green transformation as a cost burden, forward-looking companies realize that sustainable practices reduce long-term exposure to resource volatility, regulatory tightening, and reputational risks. For example, companies that invest in renewable energy not only reduce their carbon footprint but also insulate themselves from the unpredictability of fossil fuel markets. Similarly, those that redesign supply chains with circular economy principles decrease dependency on scarce raw materials while simultaneously lowering waste management costs. These shifts are not cosmetic adjustments but structural advantages that allow companies to stabilize operations and improve margins in volatile environments. Investors and financial institutions are increasingly factoring such resilience into their assessments, rewarding companies that can demonstrate alignment with environmental, social, and governance standards. In this sense, sustainability becomes not only a differentiator in customer markets but also in capital markets, where access to funding is crucial for growth and innovation. The global regulatory landscape further amplifies the role of green transformation as a competitive advantage. Governments, supranational institutions, and regional alliances are tightening standards and enforcing compliance with unprecedented rigor. Whether it is carbon pricing, emissions limits, or mandatory disclosures, businesses that proactively integrate sustainability are better positioned to comply without disruption. Moreover, these companies are often the ones shaping the regulatory agenda by collaborating with policymakers and demonstrating scalable solutions. By staying ahead of compliance requirements, they save on penalties, avoid operational halts, and gain credibility as industry standard-setters. This leadership translates into preferential treatment in partnerships, trade agreements, and government contracts, reinforcing the competitive edge derived from early adoption and proactive adaptation. Global supply chains are another arena where green transformation proves decisive. As industries become more interconnected, a company's ability to ensure sustainability across its value chain directly impacts its competitiveness. Major corporations increasingly demand that suppliers meet strict sustainability criteria as a condition for collaboration. Companies that fail to comply face exclusion from lucrative supply networks, while those that embrace sustainability enjoy not only continued access but also preferred partner status. This cascades competitive advantage across the entire ecosystem, meaning that even smaller firms must recognize the transformative power of green practices if they wish to survive in the global marketplace. For larger firms, the ability to command a sustainable supply chain strengthens reputation, enhances resilience, and aligns the brand with global standards that resonate across cultures and geographies. Beyond compliance and cost, green transformation also fosters innovation at a scale that reinvents industries. Many of the most disruptive breakthroughs in recent years have emerged from attempts to solve sustainability challenges. From plant-based alternatives to smart energy grids and biodegradable materials, green innovation opens entirely new categories of demand that never existed before. Businesses that position themselves at the forefront of such developments not only capture new revenue streams but also build intellectual property that further consolidates their market leadership. This cycle of innovation and differentiation creates barriers to entry for competitors who hesitate to embrace the transformation, ensuring that early movers enjoy sustained advantages. The competitive edge therefore lies not in doing what others are already doing but in leading the curve, defining trends before they are mainstream, and continuously adapting as science, technology, and society evolve. A significant but often underestimated dimension of competitive advantage through green transformation is the cultural and organizational renewal it inspires. Companies that embed sustainability into their core values often experience stronger employee engagement, greater retention of talent, and higher levels of innovation. Employees today seek not only compensation but also purpose, and organizations that articulate a clear sustainability vision attract individuals motivated to contribute to meaningful change. This alignment fosters creativity, accelerates collaboration, and cultivates a sense of pride that translates into higher productivity and stronger corporate culture. In competitive global labor markets, this edge in human capital is as critical as financial or technological assets. It ensures that companies are not only equipped to innovate but also resilient in the face of disruptive challenges. At the macroeconomic level, the nations and regions that prioritize sustainability are setting the stage for their domestic industries to become global leaders. Countries that invest in renewable infrastructure, sustainable agriculture, and green technologies create ecosystems that enable businesses to thrive. Companies headquartered in such regions enjoy advantages ranging from government incentives to advanced research and development clusters, giving them a head start over peers in less progressive markets. As global trade increasingly incorporates sustainability as a metric, firms from green-forward economies stand to dominate export markets and influence standards worldwide. Thus, the competitive edge of green transformation is not confined to individual companies but expands to industries, nations, and entire economic blocs that recognize the urgency of the transition. Critically, the competitive edge gained through green transformation is not static; it must be maintained through continuous evolution. Sustainability is not a milestone but a journey, and competitors are constantly catching up. Companies that treat green initiatives as one-off projects or marketing campaigns risk being overtaken by more committed and innovative players. The enduring advantage lies in cultivating adaptability, embedding sustainability into governance structures, and constantly scanning the horizon for emerging challenges and opportunities. This mindset ensures that green transformation becomes a dynamic source of competitive edge, sustaining relevance in an era where markets, technologies, and societal expectations are in perpetual flux.

The link between green transformation and massive returns becomes most visible when observing the compounding effects of all these advantages. A company that commands consumer loyalty, enjoys efficiency gains, secures investor confidence, achieves regulatory alignment, fosters innovation, and attracts top talent is positioned not only to grow but to dominate. These advantages translate into stronger financial performance, resilient market positioning, and the ability to dictate industry standards rather than merely adapting to them. Competitors that fail to keep pace are left behind, while leaders that embrace green transformation extend their influence across global markets. The sustainable advantage therefore becomes both a shield against risks and a sword for seizing opportunities, generating returns that are not just financial but reputational and strategic. In the final analysis, green transformation is not an optional strategy but a defining imperative of the twenty-first century global economy. The companies that understand this and act decisively will not merely participate in markets; they will shape them. They will not merely survive disruptions; they will create them. And they will not merely deliver quarterly profits; they will build legacies that endure across generations. The competitive edge derived from sustainability is therefore the ultimate differentiator in global markets, transforming disruption into dominance and responsibility into massive returns.

CHAPTER FOUR

The Economics of Green Capital and Sustainable Investment

The economics of green capital and sustainable investment represents one of the most transformative shifts in the financial markets of the modern era and it cannot be understood simply as an ethical choice but rather as an inevitable redirection of global capital flows toward projects that balance profitability with responsibility. Green capital is not charity and it is not philanthropy, it is capital that recognizes that the risks and opportunities of the twenty first century are intrinsically linked to environmental, social, and governance realities. Investors are increasingly aware that returns cannot be sustained in a world plagued by climate change, resource depletion, regulatory upheaval, and shifting consumer values. Such sustainable investment has matured into a mainstream financial strategy, moving billions of dollars and euros and yen toward businesses that are capable of marrying innovation with long term viability. The economics of green capital begins with understanding the revaluation of risk. Traditional financial models once calculated risk largely in terms of market fluctuations, creditworthiness, and operational inefficiencies. Today, however, climate risk has entered the equation with overwhelming force. Natural disasters, rising sea levels, unpredictable weather patterns, and carbon intensive industries facing heavy regulation all represent financial exposures that investors cannot ignore. This shift has caused financial institutions to recalibrate portfolios by reducing exposure to companies with unsustainable practices and by increasing allocations to firms positioned for resilience and adaptation. As investors have internalized these risks, sustainability has evolved into a metric of stability and foresight. Companies that demonstrate green strategies are not only judged as environmentally responsible but also as less risky and therefore more attractive as long term investments. This perception directly affects valuations, share prices, and access to funding. The rise of green bonds and sustainability linked loans exemplifies this trend. Green bonds, once a niche product, have now become a trillion dollar market, providing companies and governments with capital specifically earmarked for environmentally friendly projects such as renewable energy infrastructure, sustainable agriculture, clean transport, and water conservation. Sustainability linked loans tie interest rates to the borrower's achievement of specific environmental or social targets, meaning that the cost of capital itself is now influenced by sustainability performance. This dynamic makes sustainability not just a matter of corporate social responsibility but a determinant of financial competitiveness. Investors have recognized that integrating ESG metrics into due diligence is not a distraction but a safeguard against hidden liabilities. Businesses that ignore sustainability face reputational damage, litigation risks, and regulatory penalties, all of which erode shareholder value. Conversely companies that embrace sustainable practices often enjoy premium valuations, broader investor interest, and greater access to global capital markets. The economics of green capital is also influenced by generational shifts in investor demographics. Younger investors, who will inherit the largest wealth transfer in history, consistently express a preference for values aligned investing. They are demanding that their portfolios reflect their environmental and social priorities. This is compelling wealth managers, pension funds, and institutional investors to embed ESG criteria into their products or risk losing relevance. The growing demand is forcing a structural transformation of financial markets as asset managers repackage products to align with sustainability mandates. Another critical factor is the recognition that sustainable investments are not only risk averse but also return generating. Empirical evidence shows that ESG aligned companies often outperform their peers on both financial and operational metrics. They demonstrate better governance, stronger innovation pipelines, and more resilient supply chains. Over the medium to long term this translates into higher returns, contradicting the outdated notion that sustainability sacrifices profitability. In fact many of the world's top performing funds now integrate sustainability as a core criterion. The scale of capital being redirected into green investment is also creating self-reinforcing dynamics. As more capital flows into sustainable projects costs of technologies such as wind, solar, battery storage, and electric vehicles decrease due to economies of scale. This cost reduction further accelerates adoption, making sustainable options not only preferable but often cheaper than traditional alternatives. Thus the economics of green capital fuels a virtuous cycle where capital begets innovation, innovation lowers costs, and lowered costs attract even more capital. Governments and multilateral organizations play a catalytic role in this ecosystem. Policy incentives such as carbon pricing, subsidies for renewable energy, and tax benefits for sustainable investments make green projects more financially viable and attractive. International frameworks like the Paris Agreement signal a unified direction for global policy, providing investors with confidence that regulatory environments will continue to favor sustainable outcomes.

This alignment of capital markets, policy frameworks, and consumer values represents a tectonic shift in the economics of business. Yet challenges remain. The risk of greenwashing looms large as some companies exaggerate their sustainability claims to attract capital without delivering genuine results. Investors must sharpen their ability to distinguish authentic transformation from marketing rhetoric. This requires robust reporting standards, third party verification, and regulatory oversight. Transparency becomes the currency of credibility in the green capital markets. Moreover the transition will not be smooth across all sectors. Industries are heavily reliant on fossil fuels or resource intensive models will face difficult transitions, and investors must navigate the balance between divestment from harmful industries and supporting their transformation toward sustainability. This complexity underscores the importance of nuanced strategies that do not simply punish but incentivize change. Ultimately the economics of green capital and sustainable investment reveal a profound truth about the nature of capitalism in the twenty first century. Capital is not static, it seeks the most efficient, profitable, and secure destinations. In a world defined by environmental limits and social expectations, the most efficient destinations are those aligned with sustainability. The companies, industries, and nations that understand this truth will command capital flows, dictate market standards, and generate massive returns. Those that resist will find themselves starved of funding, burdened by risk, and sidelined in the global economy. The green economy is not a future possibility, it is the present reality, and the economics of capital has shifted irreversibly in its favor.

Redesigning Industries Through Circular Innovation

Circular innovation represents the next frontier of industrial transformation, one that challenges the centuries old linear model of take make waste and replaces it with a system designed for regeneration, reuse, and resilience. At its core circular innovation asks industries to rethink value creation by designing products and services that minimize waste and maximize utility across their entire lifecycle. This is not merely an environmental philosophy but an industrial strategy with immense economic implications. The traditional linear model was successful in driving mass production and consumption during the industrial age, but it was built on the assumption of infinite resources and an endless capacity to absorb waste. Today those assumptions have collapsed under the weight of ecological reality. Scarcity of raw materials, rising waste disposal costs, and growing consumer backlash against unsustainable practices are forcing industries to rethink their operating logic. Circular innovation offers a pathway to not only mitigate these challenges but to transform them into opportunities for profitability and growth. The first principle of circular innovation is design for durability and reuse. Products must be engineered not for planned obsolescence but for extended life cycles. This shift creates new business models where companies retain ownership of products and offer them as services, enabling them to recover and refurbish items multiple times. For example technology firms are moving toward device as a service models where consumers pay for usage rather than outright ownership. This allows companies to reclaim devices, recycle components, and resell refurbished units, generating recurring revenue streams while reducing waste. The second principle is designing disassembly and recyclability. Products should be modular, easy to take apart, and composed of materials that can be recycled without degradation. This principle not only conserves resources but also lowers production costs by ensuring that valuable materials remain in circulation. Industries such as automotive and electronics are already experimenting with modular design, enabling components to be replaced or upgraded without discarding the entire product. This extends product lifecycles, reduces costs for consumers, and creates secondary markets that further enhance profitability. Another cornerstone of circular innovation is the valorization of waste as a resource. In a circular economy waste is not discarded but repurposed into new inputs. Industrial symbiosis, where the byproducts of one industry serve as raw materials for another, exemplifies this approach. For instance agricultural waste can be converted into bioenergy, construction debris can be recycled into new building materials, and textile scraps can be transformed into new fabrics. These strategies not only reduce environmental burden but also create new revenue streams. Circular innovation thus redefines waste management from a cost center to a profit driver. The economic opportunities of circular innovation extend across entire industries. Fashion companies embracing circular practices are pioneering clothing rental models, resale platforms, and fabric recycling technologies. These not only respond to consumer demand for sustainable fashion but also generate recurring revenues and reduce dependence on volatile raw material markets. In food industries circular innovation is enabling the conversion of food waste into biofertilizers, animal feed, and even renewable energy sources. These innovations reduce costs, mitigate supply chain risks, and create new categories of products. The automotive industry is exploring remanufacturing models where used parts are refurbished to as new standards and resold, creating lower cost alternatives while minimizing environmental impact. Digital technologies amplify the potential of circular innovation. The rise of blockchain, artificial intelligence, and the Internet of Things provides the tools to track products throughout their lifecycle, optimize usage patterns, and ensure accountability in recycling processes. Smart sensors embedded in products can signal when maintenance is needed, extending lifespans and reducing premature disposal. Blockchain can ensure transparency in material sourcing and recycling, building trust with consumers and investors. Artificial intelligence can optimize reverse logistics systems, ensuring efficient collection, sorting, and redistribution of used products. Circular innovation also drives competitiveness by aligning with consumer values. As consumers increasingly demand sustainable solutions, businesses that offer circular products gain differentiation in crowded markets. They cultivate loyalty among environmentally conscious customers while attracting new demographics seeking affordability through refurbished or shared models. This consumer alignment strengthens brand equity and supports premium pricing. Moreover circular innovation fosters resilience in supply chains. By reducing dependency on virgin raw materials and extending product lifecycles, companies insulate themselves from resource volatility and geopolitical risks. This resilience is particularly valuable in industries exposed to fluctuating commodity markets or international trade disruptions. The adoption of circular innovation is not without challenges. It requires significant investment in research, redesign, and infrastructure. It also demands cultural change within organizations, as teams must shift from linear mindsets to regenerative thinking. However these challenges are outweighed by the long term gains of cost savings, risk reduction, and new revenue creation. Policymakers can accelerate adoption by implementing regulations and incentives that favor circular practices. Extended producer responsibility laws, for example, hold manufacturers accountable for the entire lifecycle of their products, incentivizing design for recyclability and reuse. Subsidies for recycling infrastructure, tax breaks for circular business models, and stricter waste regulations can further propel the shift. Investors are beginning to recognize circular innovation as a key growth driver, directing capital toward companies pioneering regenerative business models. The broader macroeconomic impact of circular innovation is profound. By keeping materials in circulation and reducing dependency on extraction, circular economies can decouple growth from resource consumption. This enables nations to pursue economic expansion without breaching ecological limits. It also reduces reliance on imports of raw materials, strengthening economic sovereignty. In a world where sustainability is increasingly tied to competitiveness, circular innovation is not just an industrial necessity but a national strategy. Ultimately the power of circular innovation lies in its ability to transform disruption into opportunity. It does not simply minimize harm but actively creates value by turning challenges into resources and limitations into innovations. The industries that embrace this paradigm will not only achieve sustainability but will secure enduring competitive advantage in global markets. The linear model has reached its limits, and the circular model stands ready to redefine the very foundations of industrial growth.

Technology, Data, and the Infrastructure of the Green Economy

The infrastructure of the green economy is being built upon a foundation of technology and data that enables unprecedented levels of efficiency, transparency, and innovation. Technology provides the tools to decarbonize industries, reduce waste, and optimize resource usage while data provides the insights necessary to make these tools effective at scale. Together they form the backbone of a new economic architecture that is not only sustainable but also more competitive and resilient. Renewable energy technologies represent one of the most visible pillars of the green economy. Solar, wind, hydro, and geothermal energy are rapidly replacing fossil fuels as the dominant sources of power. The declining costs of renewable technologies coupled with advances in energy storage are making clean energy not just an environmental choice but an economic imperative. Large scale solar farms, offshore wind installations, and next generation batteries enabling reliable and affordable power grids that can support industrial growth without compromising ecological stability. These technologies are supported by digital innovations such as smart grids, which use real time data to balance supply and demand, integrate distributed energy sources, and minimize waste. Smart grids demonstrate the interplay of technology and data, showing how infrastructure can adapt dynamically to maximize efficiency. Beyond energy the green economy relies heavily on digital technologies that improve resource management. Artificial intelligence is being applied to optimize agricultural practices, reduce water usage, and minimize the application of fertilizers and pesticides. Precision agriculture technologies employ drones, sensors, and data analytics to monitor crop health, predict yields, and guide interventions with pinpoint accuracy. This not only increases productivity but also reduces environmental impact, demonstrating how technology and data converge to align profitability with sustainability. In manufacturing, digital twins and advanced analytics allow industries to simulate processes, identify inefficiencies, and predict equipment failures before they occur. This reduces downtime, lowers energy consumption, and extends the life of assets. Predictive maintenance enabled by data driven insights ensures that resources are used optimally, costs are reduced, and waste is minimized. These applications reflect a broader truth, that sustainability is increasingly a product of intelligence as much as of intention. The infrastructure of the green economy also depends on data driven transparency in supply chains. Blockchain technology is revolutionizing traceability by allowing every step of a product's journey to be recorded, verified, and shared securely. This ensures that materials are sourced responsibly, that labor practices are ethical, and that recycling commitments are fulfilled. For businesses blockchain builds trust with consumers and investors, providing verifiable proof of sustainability claims. For regulators it provides a powerful tool to enforce standards and prevent fraud. By embedding accountability into the very fabric of commerce, data enhances both competitiveness and responsibility. Another critical area where technology drives the green economy is mobility. Electric vehicles, autonomous transportation systems, and smart logistics are redefining how goods and people move. The shift to electric vehicles supported by advances in battery technology is reducing dependence on fossil fuels and cutting urban emissions. Autonomous systems guided by artificial intelligence promise to optimize traffic flows, reduce accidents, and minimize fuel consumption. Smart logistics powered by data analytics and the Internet of Things ensures efficient routing, real time tracking, and reduced delivery times, creating both economic and environmental value. The construction and urban planning sectors are also being revolutionized by green technologies. Smart buildings equipped with sensors, automation systems, and energy efficient materials minimize resource use while maximizing comfort and functionality. Data driven urban planning enables cities to optimize land use, manage traffic congestion, and improve waste management. Green infrastructure such as vertical gardens, permeable pavements, and urban forests enhances climate resilience while improving quality of life for citizens. These innovations reflect how technology and data are not only transforming industries but also shaping the very environments in which we live and work. Finance too is being reshaped by technology in the service of the green economy. Fintech platforms are enabling fractional ownership of renewable assets, democratizing access to sustainable investments. Artificial intelligence is being used to assess ESG performance with greater precision, guiding capital toward genuinely sustainable companies. Digital platforms connect consumers directly with renewable energy providers, accelerating adoption and bypassing traditional intermediaries. By integrating technology into finance, the green economy gains speed, scale, and inclusivity. A deeper layer of transformation lies in the integration of data driven decision making into governance structures. Governments and corporations alike are using big data to model climate scenarios, assess risks, and design adaptive strategies. These models inform policies, regulations, and business strategies that are grounded in evidence rather than speculation. For businesses this means that sustainability is no longer guided by intuition alone but by precise metrics that measure carbon footprints, resource usage, and social impact. The capacity to track, report, and improve on these metrics becomes a competitive advantage in markets where accountability is prized. The expansion of digital infrastructure is therefore as critical to the green economy as physical infrastructure. High speed internet, cloud computing, and edge computing enable the collection, processing, and analysis of massive datasets that power sustainability innovations. Without robust digital connectivity, many green technologies cannot achieve scale. This makes investment in digital infrastructure a foundational requirement for the green economy, and governments that prioritize it provide their industries with significant competitive advantages. Yet as with every transformative force challenge must be addressed. The deployment of technology itself consumes energy and resources, raising questions about the sustainability of digital expansion. Data centers, for example, are energy intensive, and the proliferation of devices creates electronic waste. To ensure that technology remains a driver of the green economy, these challenges must be met with equally innovative solutions. Energy efficient data centers, circular practices in electronics manufacturing, and the development of low impact materials are essential for aligning digital growth with ecological responsibility. Another challenge is ensuring equitable access. The benefits of green technologies and data driven insights must not be limited to advanced economies or large corporations. Small businesses, developing nations, and underserved communities must also have access to the tools and knowledge that enable sustainability. This requires policies that promote inclusivity, financial mechanisms that lower barriers to entry, and collaborations that share expertise across borders. The green economy will only achieve its full potential if it is both sustainable and inclusive. Ultimately technology and data are not merely enablers of the green economy, they are its infrastructure. They provide the tools, insights, and systems that make sustainability scalable, measurable, and profitable. They transform aspirations into actionable strategies and ideals into competitive advantages. As industries, governments, and societies continue to integrate technology and data into their operations, the green economy will mature into the dominant model of global growth. The companies that master this integration will not only thrive but will define the standards of competitiveness in the twenty first century.

CHAPTER FIVE

From Local Success to Global Sustainability Transformation

S caling green innovation from local success stories to global movements requires a detailed understanding of the dynamics that govern ecosystems, industries, policies, and consumer behavior on multiple levels. A local project may emerge as a symbol of success within a confined community, but the question that defines its ultimate legacy lies in whether it can transcend boundaries and create widespread sustainable impact. When businesses innovate with green strategies, their first point of application is usually narrow, such as one factory optimizing energy use or a small city transitioning to renewable-powered transport. However, for these changes to matter in the global context of climate urgency, they must grow beyond these boundaries. This process is both technical and cultural, involving scaling strategies, partnerships, funding models, and global frameworks that ensure adaptability across geographies. The challenge with scaling is that it often confronts differences in infrastructure readiness, consumer adoption levels, policy incentives, and cultural attitudes toward sustainability. A technology that thrives in Scandinavia with robust clean energy infrastructure may face challenges in a developing economy where grids remain unstable and investments in green systems lag. This highlights that scaling is not merely about duplicating a solution but about adapting the essence of innovation to new contexts. True scaling also requires businesses to view sustainability not as a corporate side project but as a growth pillar aligned with market expansion. When a green innovation is seen as central to growth rather than an accessory, it is funded, promoted, and measured with the same rigor as traditional business growth initiatives. A classic example lies in the global spread of electric mobility. Early adopters in developed countries showed that consumers would indeed transition from combustion to battery-driven vehicles if range, convenience, and cost were addressed. However, companies like Tesla or BYD did not stop at local validation but invested in global infrastructure, such as supercharging networks, battery manufacturing plants in multiple countries, and cross-border partnerships. This demonstrates that scaling requires a system-building mindset. Governments also play a catalytic role. International agreements like the Paris Climate Accord create frameworks that push local innovation toward global adoption, but the real momentum emerges when industries align their interests with government incentives, subsidies, and penalties. For instance, solar power did not simply rise because of technological progress; it scaled massively because governments subsidized installation, incentivized production, and penalized emissions-heavy alternatives. Yet scaling is not without resistance. Incumbent industries may fight aggressively to preserve the status quo. Fossil fuel giants have historically lobbied against renewable expansion, while manufacturers invested in outdated systems often resist upgrading to cleaner technologies due to upfront costs. Overcoming such resistance requires not only technological superiority but also narrative power. Consumers, activists, and governments must be persuaded that the green innovation is not only environmentally superior but economically inevitable. Companies that succeed at scaling sustainability are those that build a strong economic case alongside the environmental one. Once it becomes financially irresponsible to resist a green transition, industries shift rapidly. Globalization has accelerated the spread of sustainable disruption because markets are more interconnected than ever. A carbon regulation in Europe affects supply chains in Asia and Africa, compelling suppliers worldwide to comply. This interconnectedness means that once a critical mass adopts a green practice, global standards shift, forcing laggards to adapt or lose access to markets. Businesses that anticipate these waves position themselves as leaders rather than reluctant followers. Ultimately, moving from local to global sustainability transformation requires vision and execution that see beyond borders. It requires building models flexible enough to adapt yet strong enough to maintain integrity. It requires creating systems that integrate local peculiarities without losing sight of global urgency. And most importantly, it requires patience and persistence, because while local success can be rapid, global transformation demands endurance, collaboration, and relentless pursuit of alignment across markets.

Financing the Expansion of Sustainable Innovation

The question of financing sits at the heart of scaling any innovation, particularly green strategies which often require significant upfront investments in infrastructure, research, and distribution. Unlike conventional businesses where growth may be funded through predictable revenue reinvestment, sustainable innovation often needs blended financing models that bring together private capital, public funding, and impact-driven investment. At the early stages, many green innovations are too risky or unproven to attract mainstream financial institutions, which tend to prefer predictable cash flows and collateral-heavy lending. This creates what is often termed the green finance gap. To close this gap, businesses must explore creative capital models. Venture capital plays an important role, but impact investors and green funds increasingly lead the way in financing sustainability ventures. These investors measure success not only by returns but by measurable reductions in emissions, waste, or resource use. A green startup working on carbon capture technology, for example, may not deliver immediate profits but will secure funding if it demonstrates scalable impact that aligns with climate targets. Beyond venture capital, partnerships with governments are crucial. Many governments offer grants, tax incentives, or low-interest loans to companies pursuing sustainable disruption. Multilateral development banks also finance large-scale projects such as renewable energy plants, water treatment systems, and clean transportation networks, particularly in emerging economies where private investors may hesitate. Green bonds have emerged as a powerful instrument in this context. These are debt securities issued to fund environmentally beneficial projects, and they have seen explosive growth in the last decade. For large corporations, issuing green bonds signals commitment to sustainability and provides capital at competitive rates due to strong investor demand for ESG-aligned assets. Furthermore, as institutional investors such as pension funds and sovereign wealth funds integrate sustainability mandates, they increasingly channel trillions of dollars into green finance opportunities. Another important model is public-private partnerships where risks and rewards are shared. For instance, a city government may co-finance renewable bus fleets with private manufacturers, or an agricultural cooperative may co-develop sustainable irrigation systems with international donors. Such blended models accelerate adoption and reduce the burden on any single entity. Businesses also need to master storytelling to attract capital.

Investors are not only drawn to spreadsheets but to compelling visions of how innovation will transform markets and lives. Entrepreneurs who communicate sustainability as a pathway to both profit and purpose stand a higher chance of securing funding. Transparency and accountability are also critical, since greenwashing concerns make investors cautious. Companies must provide robust reporting on sustainability metrics, backed by third-party audits, to maintain credibility. Financing expansion is not just about raising money but about creating a resilient capital ecosystem that can sustain innovation through cycles of uncertainty. Economic downturns, political changes, or market volatility can threaten green projects if they are overdependent on one financing channel. Diversification of capital sources, from philanthropy to revenue reinvestment to green financial instruments, ensures resilience. Ultimately, scaling sustainable innovation depends on aligning financial systems with ecological imperatives. When markets recognize that long-term prosperity is impossible without sustainability, capital flows naturally into green disruption. The companies that prepare for this inevitability by building trust with financiers, diversifying capital, and demonstrating measurable impact will be the ones to lead the next global wave of transformation.

Building Alliances for Widespread Impact

No single business, government, or community can scale sustainability alone. Green innovation achieves its fullest impact only when networks of actors across industries, regions, and sectors align to create ecosystems of change. Building alliances is therefore not an optional strategy but a necessity for widespread impact. Alliances allow companies to share resources, distribute risks, pool knowledge, and influence policy more effectively than any single actor could alone. For instance, when technology companies collaborate on renewable energy procurement through joint power purchase agreements, they create demand large enough to shift utility providers toward clean generation. In agriculture, alliances between cooperatives, suppliers, and governments help create sustainable value chains that extend from smallholder farms to global supermarkets. The foundation of strong alliances is shared purpose. Partnerships built only on transactional benefits often collapse when challenges arise, but those built on shared values and long-term goals endure. For sustainability, this means aligning around climate targets, resource efficiency, and social equity rather than narrow short-term profit. Cross-sector alliances are particularly powerful. Businesses bring capital and innovation, governments provide policy frameworks, civil society adds accountability, and academia contributes research. When these forces converge, breakthroughs occur that no single actor could achieve alone. A clear example lies in the development of the hydrogen economy. No single company or government could shoulder the immense costs and risks of building hydrogen infrastructure, but through international consortia, resources are pooled, standards are set, and markets are created collectively. Digital platforms have further transformed alliance-building by enabling collaboration across distances and industries. Open-source sustainability solutions allow companies to contribute to and benefit from collective knowledge, while blockchain enables transparent tracking of supply chains to ensure ethical practices. However, alliances are not without challenges. Differences in priorities, cultures, and governance structures can create friction. For alliances to succeed, they require mechanisms for conflict resolution, transparent decision-making, and equitable sharing of benefits. Trust must be cultivated intentionally through open communication and consistent delivery on commitments. Another challenge lies in balancing competition and cooperation. Businesses are naturally competitive, but in sustainability, pre-competitive collaboration often benefits all. For example, apparel companies collaborating on sustainable cotton sourcing or tech giants working together on recyclable materials still compete in the marketplace but cooperate in building foundational systems that benefit the industry and planet. Alliances also enhance legitimacy. When a company acts alone, its sustainability claims may be met with skepticism, but when part of a credible alliance, its actions gain validation. Consumers and regulators are more likely to trust efforts backed by coalitions of diverse actors. On a global level, alliances help align local innovations with international goals. A startup working on clean cooking stoves in Africa may lack global reach but through alliances with NGOs, governments, and international agencies, its innovation can spread to millions of households across continents. To achieve widespread impact, businesses must cultivate alliance-building as a core competency, investing not just in technologies and markets but in relationships and governance structures that enable collective action. Ultimately, sustainability is a collective challenge requiring collective solutions. Alliances transform isolated efforts into movements, local victories into global standards, and green innovations into engines of systemic change. The companies and leaders that master the art of building alliances will not only scale their impact but will shape the future of sustainable disruption for generations.

CHAPTER SIX

Technology, Policy, and Culture in Sustainable Disruption

The path toward sustainable disruption is inseparable from the rapid evolution of technology. Emerging technologies provide the tools, infrastructure, and capabilities that enable businesses, governments, and societies to not only reimagine existing systems but also build entirely new ones that prioritize ecological balance while delivering economic returns. When evaluating the role of technology in driving a greener future, it is necessary to understand that innovation is not limited to creating novel devices or platforms but also involves rethinking the integration of data, systems, and processes that unlock efficiencies at a scale once thought impossible. Consider artificial intelligence, which has become one of the most transformative enablers of sustainability in the twenty first century. AI systems allow businesses to optimize energy grids, forecast renewable power output, enhance logistics, and reduce waste across industries. By processing massive data sets, AI enables predictive maintenance for wind turbines, smart irrigation systems in agriculture, and real time monitoring of emissions in manufacturing plants. The potential extends beyond efficiency toward fundamentally reshaping how resources are consumed, redistributed, and conserved. Similarly, the Internet of Things connects billions of sensors across infrastructure, vehicles, and devices, creating intelligent ecosystems where every object becomes a data point for decision making. In cities, IoT enables smart lighting systems that adjust to human movement, waste bins that signal collection requirements, and transport systems that minimize fuel use. On a global scale, connected supply chains supported by IoT allow companies to track and verify the sustainability credentials of every component, increasing transparency and accountability. Renewable energy technologies are another cornerstone of green disruption. Advances in solar panels, wind turbines, geothermal systems, and energy storage are rapidly pushing the world toward clean power dominance. For decades, the primary barrier was cost, but the dramatic fall in renewable prices has now positioned clean energy as the cheapest source of power in many markets. Energy storage innovations, particularly in battery technologies, address intermittency challenges, enabling renewables to compete with and even surpass fossil fuel reliability. Beyond energy generation, new frontiers such as hydrogen fuel, carbon capture, and bioengineering extend the scope of technological solutions. Hydrogen, when produced through green processes, promises to decarbonize heavy industries like steelmaking and aviation where electrification remains difficult. Carbon capture technologies, though still expensive, demonstrate potential for neutralizing emissions at scale, turning waste carbon into valuable raw materials. Biotechnology reimagines agriculture through lab grown meat, genetically optimized crops, and bio based plastics that degrade naturally, all of which reduce pressure on ecosystems. Digital technologies also reshape consumer behavior. Mobile applications encourage recycling, platforms enable car sharing and circular economy participation, while blockchain provides transparency in ethical sourcing. These tools connect individual choices to systemic sustainability in ways that foster widespread adoption. However, technology alone is not sufficient. Emerging innovations must be deployed with deliberate strategies that consider equity, accessibility, and cultural contexts. The risk of widening digital divides is real, particularly if green technologies remain concentrated in wealthier regions. To truly harness technology for a greener future, diffusion must be inclusive, ensuring that developing economies benefit from innovations rather than lag behind or become dumping grounds for outdated systems. Collaboration between technology companies, governments, and civil society is critical to ensure that sustainability-driven innovation avoids unintended consequences such as e waste accumulation or displacement of vulnerable communities. Ultimately, technology is the lever of transformation, but its direction and effectiveness depend on the values, systems, and frameworks within which it operates. The companies and nations that align emerging technologies with sustainability goals will not only lead the green revolution but also define the future trajectory of human progress.

The Role of Policy in Shaping Green Markets

Policy serves as the invisible hand that shapes the direction, pace, and scope of sustainable disruption. While businesses innovate and technologies advance, the frameworks established by governments and international institutions often determine whether such innovations thrive, stagnate, or disappear. Policy creates the enabling environment in which markets operate, and in the context of sustainability, it serves as both a carrot and stick, rewarding green innovation while penalizing practices that harm the planet. The most direct form of policy intervention is regulation. Governments enforce emissions standards, ban harmful materials, and mandate efficiency targets across industries. These regulatory measures set minimum thresholds that push companies toward sustainability. For instance, the European Union has banned single use plastics and established aggressive automotive emission standards that compel manufacturers to innovate or exit the market. Regulations may initially appear restrictive, but they often catalyze competitive innovation by forcing companies to find new solutions. Beyond regulation, incentives play a powerful role. Tax credits for renewable energy, subsidies for electric vehicles, and grants for research into sustainable materials lower the cost barriers for businesses and consumers alike. These incentives reduce risk for early adopters and accelerate market penetration of green solutions. For example, the rapid growth of solar power in countries like Germany and China was directly supported by feed in tariffs and government subsidies that made adoption financially viable. Policy also influences capital flows. By setting requirements for environmental, social, and governance disclosures, governments compel financial institutions to integrate sustainability into investment decisions. Green bonds, climate funds, and carbon pricing mechanisms are examples of how policy redirects capital toward sustainable innovation. Carbon pricing in particular internalizes the environmental costs of pollution, making fossil fuel intensive industries less attractive while rewarding low carbon alternatives. International cooperation extends the power of policy beyond national borders. Agreements such as the Paris Climate Accord align countries toward common climate goals and establish frameworks for monitoring and accountability. While enforcement remains a challenge, these agreements signal to markets that sustainability is no longer optional but central to long term competitiveness. However, policy effectiveness is contingent upon enforcement and political will. Weak implementation, corruption, or inconsistent leadership can undermine even the most ambitious frameworks. Businesses must therefore not only respond to policy but also engage in shaping it. Corporate lobbying often carries a negative reputation, but when aligned with sustainability objectives, it can accelerate positive change. Industry coalitions advocating renewable standards or circular economy regulations demonstrate that business voices can push policy in the right direction. A nuanced aspect of policy is its ability to shape cultural narratives. When governments highlight sustainability as a national priority, they influence public discourse, education systems, and societal values. This cultural shift reinforces market adoption by making green practices socially desirable and politically non-negotiable. Policy is thus not only about rules and incentives but about vision and leadership. It signals direction, creates confidence, and aligns actors across society toward common goals. As climate urgency intensifies, policy will increasingly serve as the decisive force that determines whether green innovation remains fragmented or becomes the dominant paradigm of global markets.

Cultural Transformation as the Engine of Lasting Change

While technology and policy are powerful, neither can achieve lasting sustainability without cultural transformation. Culture shapes how societies value nature, consume resources, and respond to change. It influences individual behavior as much as collective decisions, determining whether innovations and policies take root or remain surface level. The deepest disruptions occur not when technologies are imposed or policies mandated but when cultural values shift to embrace sustainability as an intrinsic part of identity and progress. Cultural transformation begins with awareness. Over the past decades, movements led by activists, scientists, and media have raised global consciousness about environmental degradation, climate change, and resource scarcity. Documentaries, social media campaigns, and grassroots mobilization have brought abstract scientific data into the everyday language of ordinary citizens. This growing awareness lays the foundation for cultural change, but awareness alone is insufficient. Transformation requires the embedding of sustainability into social norms, practices, and aspirations. Education systems play a central role in shaping long term cultural perspectives. By integrating environmental literacy into curricula from early childhood through higher education, societies nurture generations that instinctively value ecological balance. Businesses contribute by aligning brands with sustainability narratives that resonate with consumers. When sustainable choices are marketed not as sacrifices but as symbols of modernity and responsibility, cultural momentum accelerates. Cultural transformation also manifests through lifestyle changes. Urban populations embrace public transportation, plant based diets gain popularity, and sharing economies replace ownership models. These shifts may begin with niche groups but spread rapidly when supported by aspirational branding and peer influence. For example, electric vehicles gained cultural momentum not only because of policy incentives but because they became associated with innovation, status, and environmental stewardship. Importantly, cultural transformation must be inclusive. In some regions, sustainability is perceived as a luxury concern disconnected from the realities of poverty or survival. To counter this, sustainability must be framed as directly improving livelihoods by reducing energy costs, enhancing health, and creating jobs. When cultural narratives highlight tangible benefits, even marginalized communities embrace change. The role of leadership in cultural transformation cannot be overstated. Visionary leaders in politics, business, and civil society inspire societies by articulating futures where prosperity and sustainability are inseparable. Cultural icons, from celebrities to influencers, also amplify messages, shaping aspirations at scale. However, cultural transformation is not always linear. Resistance often emerges when sustainable practices challenge entrenched habits, traditions, or power structures. Overcoming resistance requires empathy, dialogue, and gradual integration rather than top down imposition. The most enduring cultural changes are those that emerge organically, reinforced by multiple touchpoints in daily life. Over time, cultural transformation creates feedback loops that sustain policy and technology adoption. As citizens demand greener products, businesses respond with innovation. As businesses innovate, policies evolve to support broader adoption. As policies and innovations gain traction, cultural narratives shift further, embedding sustainability deeper into collective identity. Ultimately, culture is the engine of lasting change because it defines what societies aspire to be. When sustainability becomes a cultural cornerstone, it no longer requires enforcement or incentives but emerges as the natural course of progress. The true test of sustainable disruption is therefore not only in deploying technologies or enacting policies but in cultivating cultures that view ecological balance as integral to human flourishing.

CHAPTER SEVEN

Redefining Value and Measuring Success in Green Innovation

The definition of profitability has long been anchored in financial performance, measured by revenues, margins, and shareholder returns, yet in an era of sustainable disruption this narrow approach no longer captures the full scope of value creation. Businesses must now rethink profitability through sustainable metrics that account not only for economic gain but also for ecological preservation and social contribution. The idea of the triple bottom line emerged decades ago as an attempt to expand corporate performance into three dimensions people, planet, and profit yet in practice many firms continued to privilege financial results over all else. To truly integrate sustainability into profitability requires moving beyond symbolic gestures to recalibrating the very instruments by which businesses measure success. Sustainable metrics begin with quantifying environmental impact. Companies must assess their carbon emissions, water usage, energy efficiency, and waste management with the same rigor they apply to financial accounting. This shift reframes environmental stewardship from a peripheral corporate responsibility initiative into a core determinant of profitability. For instance, when energy efficiency reduces operating costs, emissions decline while margins expand, creating direct financial benefits from ecological responsibility. Similarly, sustainable supply chains not only reduce risks associated with resource scarcity but also enhance brand reputation and resilience. Beyond environmental factors, social metrics are critical. Fair labor practices, diversity and inclusion, community engagement, and product safety all contribute to long term value creation. Businesses that mistreat workers, exploit vulnerable populations, or neglect safety may achieve short term profits but face reputational damage, legal liabilities, and consumer backlash that erode long term viability. Conversely, companies that invest in social capital build trust and loyalty, which translate into durable profitability. Measuring profitability through sustainable metrics also requires rethinking time horizons. Traditional financial metrics often emphasize quarterly performance, but sustainability unfolds over years or decades. Investments in renewable infrastructure, circular economy systems, or ecosystem restoration may take longer to yield financial returns, but they secure resilience and relevance in the long term. By expanding time horizons, businesses align profitability with enduring value rather than transient gains. Investors are increasingly reinforcing this shift. Institutional investors now demand environmental, social, and governance disclosures and allocate capital to companies that demonstrate credible commitments to sustainability. This reshapes profitability by linking access to capital with sustainable practices. Green bonds, ESG funds, and climate aligned investments reflect a growing consensus that profitability cannot be divorced from planetary and social health. However, integrating sustainable metrics into profitability is not without challenges. Measuring non-financial impact is complex, requiring new methodologies, standards, and verification processes. Metrics must be consistent, transparent, and comparable to avoid greenwashing and build stakeholder trust.

International standards such as the Global Reporting Initiative, the Sustainability Accounting Standards Board, and the Task Force on Climate Related Financial Disclosures are emerging as frameworks to guide this process, but adoption remains uneven. Companies must also reconcile tradeoffs between short term costs and long term gains. Transitioning to sustainable production may initially raise expenses, creating pressure in competitive markets. Yet those that persevere gain advantages as regulatory landscapes tighten, consumer preferences shift, and unsustainable competitors falter. Rethinking profitability also transforms corporate governance. Boards and executives must align incentives with sustainable performance by linking compensation to ESG outcomes alongside financial metrics. This ensures that leaders prioritize holistic value creation rather than narrow financial optimization. Ultimately, profitability redefined through sustainable metrics acknowledges that businesses operate within ecological and social systems rather than outside them. True profitability arises when companies generate financial returns while preserving ecosystems and empowering communities. In this redefined model, success is measured not only by what a company extracts but by what it contributes, not only by shareholder wealth but by stakeholder well-being. This shift is not merely a moral imperative but a strategic necessity in an age where sustainability determines competitiveness, legitimacy, and survival.

Measuring Impact Beyond Traditional Returns

Measuring impact beyond traditional financial returns represents one of the most significant transformations in how businesses evaluate success in the age of sustainable disruption. Traditional returns capture profit margins, return on investment, and market share, but they fail to encompass the broader consequences of business activity on society and the environment. In a world confronted by climate change, inequality, and ecological degradation, stakeholders demand a more expansive accounting of value. Businesses that cling to narrow financial metrics risk irrelevance, while those that embrace broader measures of impact secure legitimacy, resilience, and future growth. Measuring impact begins with recognizing that every business leaves footprints ecological, social, and cultural. Quantifying these footprints requires systems that track emissions, resource consumption, waste generation, and biodiversity impacts alongside financial flows. Modern data technologies make such measurement increasingly feasible, as sensors, satellite imagery, and AI analytics provide granular insights into environmental performance. These tools allow companies to measure the full lifecycle impact of products from raw material extraction through manufacturing, distribution, use, and disposal. Lifecycle analysis reveals hidden costs and opportunities for innovation that traditional accounting overlooks. Social impact measurement is equally critical. Companies must assess wages, working conditions, diversity, inclusion, and contributions to community wellbeing. These factors determine social license to operate, which is as vital to long term success as financial returns. For example, companies sourcing materials from regions with poor labor practices may face consumer boycotts and regulatory penalties, erasing financial gains. Conversely, those that empower communities through fair wages and education initiatives cultivate loyalty and stability that support enduring profitability. Cultural and ethical impacts further expand the measurement landscape. The narratives businesses promote, the behaviors they normalize, and the aspirations they shape all influence cultural values. Companies that glorify unsustainable consumption perpetuate ecological harm, while those that promote responsible living contribute to cultural transformation. Measuring cultural impact is more abstract than counting emissions or wages, but it is no less important for evaluating holistic success. One of the most powerful frameworks for measuring impact beyond financial returns is the concept of shared value. Shared value recognizes that business success and societal progress are interconnected, and it emphasizes strategies that create economic value while addressing social and environmental challenges. This framework shifts measurement from isolated financial metrics to integrated outcomes that capture both profitability and positive externalities. Investors are increasingly demanding such integrated measurement. ESG metrics are now part of mainstream finance, influencing capital allocation and portfolio construction. Companies that fail to report credible ESG data risk exclusion from investment flows, while those that excel attract capital and favorable valuations. This dynamic reinforces the necessity of measuring impact broadly, as financial returns increasingly hinge on non-financial performance. Governments and regulators also play a role by mandating disclosures and creating standardized frameworks. The European Union's Corporate Sustainability Reporting Directive, for example, compels companies to disclose environmental and social impacts, ensuring transparency and comparability. Such mandates elevate non-financial metrics to the same level of importance as financial ones, embedding them into corporate accountability structures. Critics argue that measuring impact beyond financial returns dilutes focus and creates reporting burdens, yet the opposite is true. By embracing comprehensive measurement, businesses gain clarity about risks, opportunities, and long term trajectories that financial metrics alone obscure. Comprehensive measurement enables better decision making, innovation, and stakeholder alignment. The ultimate purpose of measuring impact beyond traditional returns is to ensure that businesses are judged not only by what they earn but by how they earn it, not only by profits generated but by legacies created. It signals a paradigm shift in which success is no longer defined narrowly by shareholder wealth but broadly by contributions to human and ecological flourishing. In this paradigm, measurement itself becomes a tool of transformation, guiding businesses toward practices that sustain both prosperity and the planet.

Embedding Sustainability into Corporate DNA

Embedding sustainability into corporate DNA means moving beyond surface level initiatives and integrating ecological and social responsibility into the core identity, strategy, and operations of a business. It is not about creating isolated departments or campaigns but about ensuring that every decision, process, and innovation reflects a commitment to sustainability. For many companies, sustainability begins as a response to external pressure from regulators, consumers, or activists, but true transformation occurs when it becomes intrinsic to corporate purpose. At the strategic level embedding sustainability requires aligning vision and mission statements with ecological and social goals. When sustainability is articulated as part of corporate purpose, it guides decision making across the organization. Companies such as Patagonia, which explicitly defines its mission as saving the planet, demonstrate how sustainability integrated into purpose drives consistency and authenticity. This alignment ensures that sustainability is not vulnerable to leadership changes or shifting market trends but endures as a defining feature of identity. Operational integration is the next step. Supply chains must be redesigned to prioritize renewable materials, ethical labor, and circular flows. Manufacturing processes must optimize energy efficiency and minimize waste. Product design must consider lifecycle impacts, from resource extraction to end of life disposal. Embedding sustainability requires rigorous systems for monitoring, reporting, and improving performance across these dimensions. It also requires investment in innovation to continually enhance sustainability outcomes. Cultural integration within the organization is equally important. Employees must view sustainability not as an external mandate but as part of their daily work and professional identity. Training, incentives, and leadership modeling foster a culture where sustainability becomes instinctive. When employees at all levels embrace sustainability, it permeates organizational behavior and decision making. Governance structures reinforce this integration. Boards must oversee sustainability performance with the same seriousness as financial results, and executive compensation must be tied to ESG outcomes. Accountability at the highest levels ensures that sustainability remains a strategic priority rather than a peripheral concern. Communication also plays a role. Companies must transparently report sustainability performance, acknowledging challenges as well as achievements. Authentic communication builds trust with stakeholders and reinforces internal commitment. Greenwashing undermines this trust, so embedding sustainability requires honesty, consistency, and verifiable progress. The benefits of embedding sustainability into corporate DNA are profound. It builds resilience against regulatory changes, market shifts, and resource constraints. It enhances brand reputation, attracting loyal customers and top talent. It opens access to capital from investors prioritizing ESG performance. Most importantly, it aligns corporate success with societal and planetary well-being, ensuring long term viability. The journey toward embedding sustainability is not without obstacles. It requires overcoming inertia, entrenched practices, and short term pressures. Yet companies that embrace this journey gain competitive advantages and shape the future of their industries. They transition from reactive compliance to proactive leadership, from fragmented initiatives to holistic transformation. Ultimately embedding sustainability into corporate DNA is about authenticity and permanence.

It is about creating businesses whose very existence contributes to ecological balance and social equity. In such companies' profitability and sustainability are not tradeoffs but expressions of the same purpose. This integration redefines corporate excellence for the twenty first century, establishing new standards of legitimacy, competitiveness, and legacy.

CHAPTER EIGHT

Green Technology as the Core of Competitive Advantage

The twenty first century has produced an era where technology is not only a tool for efficiency but a defining edge of survival in markets that have become more conscious, more regulated, and more interconnected than ever before. Within this shift, green technology has emerged as more than a supplemental improvement or a checkbox for corporate responsibility. It has become the very engine of competitive advantage. Companies that once believed innovation could be achieved by simply digitizing processes or automating production have come to realize that true market differentiation and long term resilience stem from embedding sustainability into the core of their technological frameworks. Green technology encompasses everything from renewable energy systems and energy efficient manufacturing to waste to resource innovations and circular business models that leverage advanced analytics and artificial intelligence to predict, optimize, and reduce ecological footprints. The firms that have leaned into these transitions are not just appealing to environmentally conscious customers. They are also future proofing themselves against rising costs of energy, global supply chain volatility, regulatory penalties, and reputational risks that can erode consumer trust. A business that can deliver more value with less resource intensity is positioned not only to reduce operational costs but to command greater market authority. When green technology becomes central to competitive advantage, companies move from being followers of sustainability trends to being creators of new market rules. They define the standards others must chase. One sees this dynamic in industries such as automotive manufacturing where electric vehicle companies disrupted giants who for decades dominated internal combustion engines. The technological pivot to electric drivetrains coupled with digital software integration became the competitive differentiator. Yet what truly secured their advantage was not only technological novelty but the sustainability narrative embedded in the very DNA of their products. Consumers bought not merely cars but identities tied to cleaner futures. The same can be observed in consumer packaged goods where brands that use biodegradable packaging supported by material science innovation are now capturing more shelf space and commanding higher price premiums because they represent responsibility without compromising quality. Investors increasingly reward these companies because their green technological foundations signal lower exposure to climate risks and higher adaptability to future resource constraints. The embedding of green technology into competitive advantage is not limited to external outcomes but also transforms internal culture. When employees are engaged in work that contributes to the mitigation of global challenges they find greater meaning and loyalty in their contributions. Talent acquisition and retention therefore become easier as the younger workforce increasingly chooses employers based on alignment with sustainable values. The integration of digital transformation with green principles creates an even stronger competitive edge. Artificial intelligence applied to energy consumption data allows companies to cut waste and optimize supply chains in ways that deliver both environmental and financial benefits. Blockchain technology supports transparent supply chains that prove ethical sourcing and minimize reputational risks in an age of heightened scrutiny. Smart manufacturing powered by the internet of things enables predictive maintenance, reducing downtime and extending equipment lifespan, thereby conserving resources and lowering costs. The compounding effects of these technologies create an ecosystem of advantages that reinforce one another. The most forward thinking firms do not treat green technology as a cost center but as a strategic investment that unlocks revenue growth, enhances brand value, and positions them as market leaders. Competitive advantage is no longer defined solely by who can produce at scale but by who can innovate at scale without compromising planetary boundaries. In this sense green technology is not an option but a prerequisite. Those who fail to embed it into their strategies will find themselves increasingly marginalized as consumers, investors, regulators, and talent align with companies that reflect the values of a sustainable future. The shift is irreversible and the race to integrate green technology as the foundation of competitive advantage has already determined the trajectory of winners and losers in this century's marketplace.

Financial Innovation for Sustainable Growth

For sustainable disruption to generate massive returns the marriage of financial innovation with ecological responsibility is indispensable. Traditional financing models often evaluate success based on short term profit maximization and linear projections of market growth. Yet sustainability requires a different lens, one that accounts for long term resilience, systemic risks, and externalities that conventional accounting frameworks often ignore. Financial innovation in the realm of green strategies redefines how capital is allocated, how returns are measured, and how stakeholders capture value. Green bonds, sustainability linked loans, carbon trading mechanisms, and impact investment funds are only the surface of a much deeper restructuring of finance. These instruments provide organizations with not only the liquidity to invest in transformative projects but also the credibility to signal seriousness to markets increasingly attentive to environmental, social, and governance performance. A company that issues green bonds to finance renewable infrastructure not only secures favorable interest rates but also attracts investors aligned with sustainability mandates. These investors are more patient, less speculative, and more likely to support long term strategies. Financial innovation in this sense creates stability in uncertain markets. Furthermore, integrating sustainability metrics into corporate finance shifts the perception of risk and opportunity. Projects that reduce carbon emissions, conserve water, or regenerate ecosystems are no longer considered external or peripheral but are core to value creation. By quantifying avoided costs such as future carbon taxes or regulatory penalties companies can demonstrate the tangible financial returns of sustainability investments. This broadens access to capital because lenders and investors now see reduced risk exposure rather than increased expense. The role of financial innovation also extends to consumer facing products. Banks and fintech companies are introducing green credit cards that incentivize sustainable purchasing, carbon offset mechanisms tied to payment platforms, and digital investment apps that allow retail investors to channel resources into clean energy funds. Such democratization of green finance ensures that sustainability is not limited to large institutional players but becomes part of everyday economic behavior. Insurance is another sector undergoing transformation as financial innovation responds to climate risks. Insurers are redesigning products to reward businesses that adopt green technologies with lower premiums while penalizing those who ignore climate adaptation strategies. This risk adjusted pricing sends powerful signals across markets by translating ecological responsibility into financial advantage. The compounding effect is that companies which innovate financially around sustainability not only secure better funding terms but also expand market share through products that align with both consumers and regulators. Importantly, financial innovation must move beyond superficial green labeling or what critics call greenwashing. To maintain credibility markets demand transparency and measurable outcomes. This has led to the rise of frameworks such as the task force on climate related financial disclosures and environmental social governance reporting standards. Companies that integrate these frameworks not only meet compliance requirements but also attract a more diverse and loyal investor base. The future of sustainable growth will not be determined solely by technological breakthroughs but by financial architectures capable of supporting their scale and diffusion. For example renewable energy technologies are already cost competitive with fossil fuels but their widespread adoption depends on financing models that reduce upfront capital barriers and enable distributed ownership structures such as community energy cooperatives. Here financial innovation transforms access and equity ensuring that sustainability is inclusive rather than exclusive. Ultimately financial innovation for sustainable growth reshapes the very definition of returns. It recognizes that profit without resilience is hollow, that growth without regeneration is unsustainable, and that capital without conscience is increasingly unacceptable to societies that bear the costs of climate degradation. By embedding these principles into their financial DNA organizations ensure that disruption becomes sustainable not only in ecological terms but in economic longevity.

Cultural Transformation and the Human Dimension of Sustainability

Technological progress and financial innovation can only go so far without the transformation of culture. Human beings ultimately design, adopt, and sustain every system. Therefore the human dimension of sustainability is both the catalyst and the anchor of disruption. Cultural transformation requires organizations to embed values of responsibility, stewardship, and long term thinking into their identity. It is not enough to introduce green technologies or finance models if the people within and around the organization continue to operate with mindsets anchored in short term extraction. Culture is the invisible infrastructure that sustains visible change. In companies that have successfully embraced sustainability one finds a consistent narrative of leadership commitment, employee engagement, and stakeholder collaboration. Leaders in these organizations do not merely communicate environmental goals in annual reports but model them in their decisions, incentives, and accountability mechanisms. Employees are not passive executors of sustainability policies but are active participants generating ideas, identifying inefficiencies, and fostering cross functional collaboration to reduce footprints. Customers are treated not as external consumers but as partners in co creating sustainable solutions. This cultural fabric enables resilience because it aligns purpose with action across every layer of the enterprise. The human dimension also extends beyond organizational boundaries into society. Businesses exist within cultural ecosystems shaped by communities, governments, and global movements. When a company champions cultural transformation it contributes to shifting social norms that redefine consumption patterns, regulatory expectations, and civic behavior. For example cultural embrace of plant based diets has accelerated market growth for alternative proteins which in turn reduces pressures on land and water resources. Similarly the rise of zero waste lifestyles has pushed retailers to offer packaging free options and redesign supply chains. In both cases cultural momentum became the force multiplier of technological and financial innovations. Resistance to sustainability often arises not from technological impossibility or financial infeasibility but from cultural inertia. People resist change when they perceive it as threatening their identity, convenience, or social standing. Therefore successful cultural transformation requires storytelling, education, and incentives that reframe sustainability as aspirational rather than sacrificial. Marketing campaigns that associate sustainable products with status, creativity, and empowerment are far more effective than those that rely solely on fear of ecological collapse. The human brain responds to narratives of hope and possibility more strongly than to doom and guilt. The cultural transformation must also be inclusive. Communities disproportionately affected by climate change or industrial pollution often lack the resources to participate in sustainable transitions. If businesses ignore these disparities they risk reinforcing inequities and losing legitimacy. By contrast organizations that actively involve marginalized groups in their sustainability strategies generate not only social justice but also untapped markets and innovation potential. Diversity of perspectives enriches problem solving and leads to solutions that are more adaptable and equitable. Within companies' cultural transformation requires structural reinforcement. Training programs, reward systems, and governance frameworks must align with sustainable values. An employee who proposes a resource saving innovation should be rewarded not sidelined. A manager who prioritizes long term environmental gains over short term profit margins should be supported not penalized. Over time these practices accumulate into cultural DNA that sustains transformation. The human dimension also intersects with mental models of growth and success. Cultures that equate success solely with material accumulation perpetuate unsustainable consumption. By contrast cultures that redefine success in terms of wellbeing, balance, and contribution to the common good enable lifestyles and business models aligned with planetary boundaries. This shift is not abstract but practical. For example companies that promote flexible working arrangements reduce commuting emissions while enhancing employee wellbeing. Those that invest in regenerative supply chains improve ecological resilience while building trust with conscious consumers. Cultural transformation therefore is not an optional soft layer but the very foundation of sustainable disruption. Without its technologies may remain underutilized and financial innovations may fail to achieve scale. With it the human imagination and collective will become the most powerful resources of all. By cultivating cultures of sustainability we unlock the creativity, resilience, and purpose necessary to generate not only massive returns but enduring legacies.

CHAPTER NINE

Policy, Regulation, and the Architecture of Sustainable Markets

The global economy is shaped not only by the innovations of businesses or the choices of consumers but by the rules and structures created through policy and regulation. These frameworks form the architecture of sustainable markets and determine the pace at which green innovation strategies can scale to generate massive returns. Without the scaffolding of regulation many industries would continue to operate with models that externalize costs to the environment and society while capturing profits for a few. Regulation internalizes these costs and ensures that markets reward those who innovate sustainably rather than those who exploit loopholes. Policies such as carbon pricing, renewable energy mandates, waste reduction targets, and emission standards provide clear signals to businesses and investors. They create certainty in markets where uncertainty has long been a barrier to investment in green technologies. When companies can anticipate that carbon will be taxed at increasing levels they have incentives to reduce their footprint proactively rather than reactively. Similarly when renewable portfolio standards guarantee market demand for clean energy producers can scale with confidence knowing there is a regulatory floor beneath them. These mechanisms are not anti-business as critics often claim but are in fact enablers of long term business resilience because they level the playing field and reward efficiency and innovation. Markets that lack robust policy frameworks often find themselves vulnerable to greenwashing where companies claim sustainability without meaningful action because there are no penalties for dishonesty or benchmarks for accountability. Regulation prevents this by requiring disclosure of environmental performance and by penalizing misrepresentation. The introduction of environmental social and governance reporting frameworks has made sustainability data as critical to investors as financial statements. This shift has been profound because it aligns fiduciary duty with ecological responsibility. Companies that fail to disclose or that underperform against ESG benchmarks face higher costs of capital while those that lead attract larger pools of investment. Regulation also plays a role in global trade. As countries adopt stricter sustainability standards they begin to impose border adjustments on imports from regions with weaker rules. This creates ripple effects across supply chains and pressures companies in all geographies to align with global standards. The European Union's carbon border adjustment mechanism for instance sends a powerful signal that carbon intensive goods will face higher costs when entering European markets. Exporters in developing economies must therefore adapt their practices or risk losing access to lucrative markets. While this may seem harsh it can also drive innovation by forcing industries to leapfrog outdated models and adopt cleaner technologies faster than they might have otherwise. Policy also shapes consumer behavior. Subsidies for electric vehicles, tax credits for solar installations, and bans on single use plastics all influence the choices consumers make. When governments align incentives with sustainability they not only make greener options more affordable but also normalize them culturally. Over time this builds momentum that drives markets to evolve even in the absence of further regulation. However policy is not without challenges. Regulatory capture where powerful industries influence policy to protect their interests remains a persistent risk. Policymakers must therefore design frameworks that are transparent, inclusive, and resilient against lobbying that undermines sustainability goals. Additionally policies must balance ambition with feasibility to avoid backlash. Sudden regulations that disrupt livelihoods without transition support can lead to social resistance and political instability. This is why transition frameworks have become central to modern climate policy ensuring that workers and communities dependent on high carbon industries are supported with retraining, investment, and social safety nets as economies shift toward sustainability. The architecture of sustainable markets is therefore a dynamic interplay between rules that constrain harmful practices and incentives that encourage innovation. It is a delicate balance that requires continuous adaptation as technologies evolve and social expectations shift. Policymakers who succeed will not only accelerate the pace of green innovation but will also secure competitive advantage for their economies on the global stage. Nations that lead in shaping sustainable regulatory frameworks will attract investment, talent, and influence while those that lag will find themselves marginalized in a future defined by ecological constraints. Regulation is often viewed as a burden but in reality it is the blueprint of opportunity because it sets the parameters within which creativity can thrive. By designing markets that reward sustainability we ensure that disruption is not chaotic but constructive and that the returns generated are not fleeting but enduring.

Scaling Innovation through Global Collaboration

The challenges of climate change and ecological degradation are global in nature and therefore the solutions must also transcend national borders. No single country or company can alone address the complexities of resource scarcity, pollution, and rising emissions. Global collaboration is the multiplier that enables innovation to scale from isolated breakthroughs to systemic transformation. Collaborative platforms that bring together governments, businesses, research institutions, and civil society create ecosystems where knowledge, technology, and capital can flow across boundaries. These ecosystems accelerate innovation by reducing duplication of effort and by spreading risk across multiple actors. When nations pool resources into global funds for clean technology deployment they not only expand access for developing economies but also drive down costs for everyone by achieving economies of scale. Similarly when companies form cross industry alliances to share best practices and co-develop standards they enable entire sectors to move forward together rather than fragment into isolated experiments. Collaboration also enhances legitimacy because solutions developed collectively are more likely to be accepted across cultures and political contexts. For example international agreements such as the Paris Climate Accord set global targets that provide direction for national policies and corporate strategies. While enforcement mechanisms may be limited the accord nonetheless establishes a shared vision that aligns diverse actors. Businesses can then innovate confidently knowing that the direction of travel is toward decarbonization even if the pace varies across regions. Collaboration is not only top down but also bottom up. Grassroots movements, non-governmental organizations, and local communities play crucial roles in shaping sustainable practices that can later be scaled globally. For instance innovations in community energy cooperatives pioneered in parts of

Europe have inspired similar models in Africa and Asia enabling rural communities to access renewable energy without waiting for centralized grid expansion. These models thrive when knowledge transfer occurs across borders supported by digital platforms and international partnerships. Technology has become an enabler of global collaboration in unprecedented ways. Digital connectivity allows researchers to collaborate in real time, businesses to manage global supply chains transparently, and consumers to mobilize pressure across continents. Open source platforms for sustainability data and tools democratize access to knowledge that once remained confined to elite institutions. This democratization accelerates innovation by allowing anyone anywhere to contribute solutions. Yet collaboration is not without barriers. Geopolitical rivalries, protectionism, and intellectual property disputes often limit the willingness of nations and corporations to share knowledge freely. To overcome these barriers trust must be built through governance structures that protect fair use and equitable benefit sharing. International organizations play an important role here by mediating disputes, setting norms, and providing neutral platforms for collaboration. The role of finance is also critical. Global collaboration often requires pooled funding mechanisms to support large scale initiatives such as renewable infrastructure projects in developing nations. Institutions like the Green Climate Fund exemplify this approach by channeling resources from wealthier nations to support sustainable transitions in vulnerable economies. This not only addresses equity concerns but also ensures that innovation scales globally rather than being confined to wealthy regions. Global collaboration also fosters resilience by diversifying sources of knowledge and technology. When solutions are developed across diverse cultural and ecological contexts they are more robust and adaptable. For example agricultural innovations developed in response to drought in one region can inform practices in another facing similar conditions. This cross pollination of ideas strengthens global capacity to respond to unpredictable challenges. Ultimately scaling innovation through global collaboration transforms sustainability from a competitive advantage for a few into a collective safeguard for humanity. It shifts the narrative from zero sum competition to positive sum cooperation where every participant gains through shared resilience. The twenty first century will be defined not only by the technological breakthroughs we achieve but by the collaborative frameworks we build to ensure that those breakthroughs reach everyone. Without collaboration innovation risks remaining fragmented and insufficient. With collaboration it becomes the foundation of a sustainable and prosperous future for all.

Leadership and Governance in a Sustainable Age

The final dimension of sustainable disruption that must be addressed is leadership and governance. The quality of leadership determines whether organizations and societies can navigate the complexities of transition and harness disruption to generate massive returns. In a sustainable age leaders must embody a different set of skills and values than those celebrated in the industrial era. They must balance profitability with responsibility, growth with regeneration, and innovation with equity. Governance structures must evolve alongside leadership to provide accountability, transparency, and inclusivity. Leadership in sustainability is not merely about setting ambitious targets or adopting green rhetoric. It is about embedding sustainability into the core mission and ensuring that every decision reflects long term ecological and social impacts. Leaders must be systems thinkers capable of seeing connections between environmental health, economic performance, and social wellbeing. They must also be adaptive learners who recognize that sustainability is a journey requiring continuous experimentation and adjustment rather than a static destination. Such leadership is not confined to individuals at the top but must be distributed across organizations. Empowering middle managers, frontline employees, and even consumers to act as leaders in their spheres creates a culture where sustainability becomes self-sustaining. Governance structures play the complementary role of ensuring that leadership commitments are not hollow promises. Boards of directors must integrate sustainability expertise into their composition. Shareholders must be engaged not only on financial returns but on long term resilience. Auditing mechanisms must track progress against sustainability goals with the same rigor as financial performance. Without governance leadership risks becoming symbolic rather than transformative. The sustainable age also demands inclusive leadership. Historically marginalized voices including indigenous communities, women, and youth often hold knowledge and perspectives vital to sustainability yet they remain underrepresented in decision making. Bringing these voices into leadership structures enriches problem solving and ensures that solutions are equitable. Governance frameworks must therefore prioritize diversity and inclusivity as core principles. Ethical leadership is equally essential. In an era where greenwashing is prevalent leaders must demonstrate integrity by aligning words with actions. Trust once lost is difficult to regain and in sustainability trust is the currency that determines legitimacy. Leaders who consistently deliver commitments build credibility that translates into consumer loyalty, investor confidence, and employee engagement. Leadership in a sustainable age also requires courage. Transitioning to sustainable models often involves challenging entrenched interests, disrupting profitable but harmful practices, and making sacrifices in the short term for long term gain. Courageous leaders are willing to confront these challenges because they understand that the cost of inaction far outweighs the discomfort of transition. The global nature of sustainability challenges further requires leaders to think beyond narrow national or corporate interests. Collaborative leadership that seeks partnerships rather than domination is necessary. Governance mechanisms at the international level such as climate accords, trade agreements, and standards bodies provide the platforms for such collaboration but they require leaders who are willing to compromise and share power for the greater good. As the world faces increasingly complex crises from climate change to biodiversity loss to inequality the need for transformative leadership has never been greater. The leaders who will be remembered are those who recognized that sustainability was not a constraint but an opportunity to redefine prosperity. Governance systems that support such leadership will be the scaffolding upon which sustainable disruption flourishes. In this sustainable age leadership is not measured solely by quarterly earnings but by the ability to generate enduring value for people, planet, and profit. The companies, nations, and institutions that embrace this model will not only survive disruption but will lead it, turning challenges into opportunities and ensuring that their legacy is one of regeneration rather than depletion.

CHAPTER TEN

Measuring Impact and Sustaining Growth in Green Innovation

S ustainable disruption cannot be sustained without measurement because what cannot be measured cannot be improved or scaled. For decades businesses relied exclusively on financial metrics to determine success, focusing on profit margins, shareholder returns, and quarterly growth while ignoring the hidden costs imposed on the environment and society. This one dimensional model of success created perverse incentives that drove ecological destruction, social inequality, and long term instability. In the age of green innovation companies must move beyond the limits of financial accounting to embrace a holistic view of value creation, one that integrates environmental and social performance alongside economic outcomes. Measuring impact in this context requires redefining success itself. Rather than asking only how much profit was made, companies must ask how much carbon was reduced, how many ecosystems were restored, how much resource efficiency was achieved, how equitably the benefits of innovation were distributed, and how well long term resilience was built. This shift is not simply about compliance with regulation or appeasing investors, it is about survival in a world where climate change, biodiversity loss, and resource scarcity directly threaten economic stability. The imperative is to create a measurement system that captures the full picture of business activity so that firms can navigate complexity with accuracy and credibility. One of the first elements of measuring green impact is carbon accounting which has emerged as the gold standard for climate reporting. Scope One emissions account for direct emissions from owned or controlled sources, Scope Two covers indirect emissions from purchased energy, and Scope Three encompasses all other indirect emissions across the value chain including suppliers and customers. Many companies previously focused only on Scope One and Two because they are easier to measure, but in reality Scope Three often represents the majority of a company's carbon footprint. Therefore accurate carbon measurement demands rigorous supply chain mapping, data collection, and collaboration with partners to uncover hidden emissions. By quantifying emissions across all scopes companies can set science based targets aligned with global climate goals and demonstrate genuine commitment to decarbonization. Beyond carbon other dimensions of impact require equal attention. Water usage and water stress indicators are critical for industries in agriculture, textiles, and manufacturing where resource depletion threatens both business continuity and local communities. Measuring waste generation, recycling rates, and circularity performance allows businesses to transition away from linear models of take make dispose towards circular economies where materials are continually reused. Biodiversity indicators capture the effect of business operations on species habitats, deforestation, and ecosystem health which are often neglected despite their critical role in planetary resilience. On the social side companies must measure workforce diversity, fair labor practices, gender equity, health and safety outcomes, and community engagement. The rise of Environmental Social and

Governance reporting has provided a framework for integrating these multiple dimensions into comprehensive disclosures. Investors increasingly rely on ESG ratings to evaluate companies not only for ethical reasons but also to assess long term risk exposure. Firms with poor ESG performance face higher regulatory risks, supply chain disruptions, and reputational damage while those with strong ESG records attract capital more easily. Measuring impact also strengthens consumer trust because today's consumers want assurance that sustainability claims are backed by evidence. Greenwashing has eroded trust in corporate messaging, so transparency through verifiable metrics has become indispensable. Measurement enhances internal decision making as well because when companies track environmental and social performance with the same rigor as financial performance they uncover inefficiencies, identify areas for innovation, and foster accountability across departments. Measurement systems encourage alignment between strategy and execution because goals become tangible and progress can be monitored. However measurement is not without challenges. Data quality remains a significant barrier as companies often lack accurate data from suppliers or face inconsistencies across geographies. The lack of standardized metrics complicates comparability across industries making it difficult for investors and regulators to evaluate performance consistently. To address these challenges firms must invest in digital technologies such as Internet of Things sensors, artificial intelligence analytics, and blockchain transparency tools that allow real time data collection and verification. Third party audits and certifications enhance credibility by providing independent verification of reported results. Measurement frameworks must also balance global comparability with local relevance since sustainability challenges vary widely depending on context. For instance water efficiency is more critical in arid regions than in areas of water abundance. A one size fits all metric would obscure important nuances so businesses must adapt frameworks to capture local realities while maintaining global alignment. Another dimension of measuring impact lies in long term horizons. Many green innovations yield benefits that accumulate over decades rather than months, yet financial reporting cycles emphasize short term outcomes. Businesses must therefore adopt long term metrics that reflect intergenerational impacts. For example investments in reforestation projects or renewable infrastructure might show limited short. term returns but over time produce immense environmental and economic benefits. Including these long term perspectives in measurement systems ensures that companies are not disincentivized from pursuing transformative projects. Ultimately measuring green impact beyond financial metrics transforms sustainability from aspiration to accountability. It ensures that companies not only claim to create value but can demonstrate how that value materializes across environmental, social, and economic dimensions. Measurement becomes a driver of competitive advantage because companies that can prove their impact will attract investors, retain loyal customers, and inspire employees. It also aligns businesses with the global shift towards regenerative economies where success is defined not only by profitability but by the flourishing of people and the planet.

Strategies for Sustaining Growth in Green Innovation Ecosystems

Sustaining growth in green innovation requires more than isolated projects or pilot programs, it demands the creation of ecosystems that continuously nurture, scale, and regenerate innovation across industries and geographies. Green innovation thrives when it is embedded in networks of stakeholders that reinforce each other's progress rather than competing in isolation. These ecosystems are dynamic systems composed of businesses, governments, investors, research institutions, and civil society working together to accelerate the transition to sustainable economies. To sustain growth in such ecosystems companies must adopt strategies rooted in systemic integration, collaboration, adaptive capacity, and inclusive value creation. Systemic integration means embedding sustainability into the core strategy and structure of an organization so deeply that it becomes inseparable from the business model. When procurement policies demand sustainable sourcing suppliers are compelled to raise their standards. When financial teams integrate climate risk into investment decisions firms avoid stranded assets and future disruptions. When human resources prioritize sustainability literacy and purpose driven recruitment the entire workforce becomes aligned with long term goals. Systemic integration ensures that sustainability is not confined to a department but drives the entire value chain. Collaboration is another cornerstone of sustained growth. No single company can solve systemic problems like climate change or biodiversity loss alone. Partnerships with competitors to establish industry wide standards, alliances with governments to co invest in infrastructure, and collaborations with universities to drive research all extend the scope and speed of innovation. Public private partnerships for renewable energy development, industry consortia for circular economy practices, and global coalitions for decarbonization all exemplify how collaboration transforms isolated efforts into collective movements. These collaborations also reduce risk because they spread responsibility across multiple actors while creating shared ownership of solutions. Adaptive capacity is vital for sustaining growth in rapidly changing landscapes. Green technologies evolve quickly, regulatory frameworks shift, and consumer expectations change. Companies must cultivate agility by continuously scanning for emerging trends, investing in flexible business models, and fostering a culture of experimentation. Adaptive firms treat failures as learning opportunities rather than setbacks and encourage employees to innovate at every level. For example companies exploring hydrogen energy, carbon capture, or regenerative agriculture must be ready to pivot as scientific knowledge and policy evolve. Those who fail to adapt risk being outpaced by competitors or rendered obsolete by disruptive breakthroughs. Financial strategies play a critical role in sustaining green growth because many innovations require significant upfront investment. Green bonds, sustainability linked loans, and blended finance mechanisms provide capital structures aligned with long term sustainability goals. Impact investors are increasingly seeking opportunities that combine financial returns with measurable social and environmental outcomes. By leveraging these financing mechanisms firms secure resources to scale innovation while signaling commitment to stakeholders. Sustaining growth also depends on authentic branding and consumer engagement. Businesses that communicate their sustainability journey transparently and consistently cultivate trust and loyalty. Consumers are more likely to remain loyal to brands that align with their values even in competitive markets. However authenticity is key because greenwashing can destroy credibility. By sharing both successes and challenges companies invite consumers to participate in the sustainability journey, creating deeper connections that sustain long term growth. Talent development is equally crucial for sustaining innovation. A workforce motivated by purpose, equipped with sustainability literacy, and empowered to innovate ensures that green strategies evolve continuously. Companies must invest in training, mentorship, and incentives that reward sustainability leadership. Younger generations especially seek purpose driven careers, so cultivating a culture of sustainability attracts and retains top talent. Without engaged and capable people even the most ambitious strategies cannot endure. Governments and policy frameworks influence the sustainability of green innovation ecosystems. Regulations that incentivize renewable energy, penalize pollution, and support circular economy models create fertile ground for innovation. Companies must proactively engage with policymakers to shape supportive frameworks while preparing to meet evolving requirements. Early adopters of high standards often gain first mover advantages and position themselves as industry leaders. Technology amplifies all these strategies by providing tools to optimize efficiency, monitor progress, and predict future challenges. Artificial intelligence enables predictive sustainability analysis, IoT devices allow real time monitoring of emissions and resource use, and blockchain ensures supply chain transparency. These technologies enhance credibility, scalability, and precision in sustainability strategies. However technology must be deployed ethically to avoid unintended consequences such as digital inequality or unsustainable energy consumption. Sustaining growth also requires inclusivity because green innovation cannot thrive if it excludes marginalized communities. Companies must design strategies that create opportunities for small businesses, local communities, and vulnerable populations. Inclusive ecosystems ensure that sustainability is not only a privilege of wealthy nations or corporations but a global movement that uplifts all. This inclusivity strengthens resilience because systems with broad participation are less fragile and more adaptive. In sum strategies for sustaining growth in green innovation ecosystems revolve around integration, collaboration, adaptability, financial innovation, authentic branding, talent development, policy engagement, technological tools, and inclusivity. By aligning these dimensions companies create ecosystems that regenerate themselves rather than deplete momentum. Sustained growth in green innovation is not a matter of luck but the outcome of intentional strategy, disciplined execution, and a collective vision that extends beyond individual firms.

Creating a Legacy of Resilient and Regenerative Business Practices

The true achievement of green innovation lies not only in the immediate outcomes it delivers but in the legacy it leaves for future generations. Creating a legacy of resilient and regenerative practices ensures that progress is not undone by external shocks or abandoned after leadership changes. Legacy in this context means embedding sustainability so deeply into business culture, governance, and identity that it endures as a living system capable of adapting, regenerating, and inspiring. Resilience is central to legacy because the future will bring inevitable disruptions from climate shocks to technological upheavals. Businesses that integrate resilience into their models can absorb shocks while continuing to deliver value. This requires diversified supply chains that reduce vulnerability to disruptions, renewable energy systems that buffer against fossil fuel volatility, and scenario planning that anticipates multiple possible futures. Resilient companies do not merely survive uncertainty, they thrive in it because they are designed to be flexible, adaptive, and forward looking. Regeneration elevates legacy beyond resilience because it seeks not only to withstand challenges but to restore and enhance systems. Regenerative practices replenish natural resources, strengthen social equity, and enhance community wellbeing. For example regenerative agriculture rebuilds soil fertility, improves water retention, and increases biodiversity, leaving ecosystems healthier than before. Regenerative business models design products for disassembly and reuse, ensuring that resources are continually cycled back into production. Regeneration transforms businesses from extractive entities into restorative institutions that actively improve the systems on which they depend. A legacy of regenerative practices also requires cultural transformation within organizations. Leadership can initiate the vision but the entire workforce must embody the mission.

Shared values, rituals, and narratives embed sustainability into the organizational identity so that it persists across leadership transitions. Training and education ensure that employees at all levels understand and contribute to sustainability goals. When sustainability becomes part of the culture employees act as stewards of the legacy, carrying it forward with commitment and creativity. External influence is another dimension of legacy because companies that lead in sustainability set benchmarks for entire industries. By raising standards, inspiring competitors, and influencing policy they create ripple effects that multiply their impact. For instance a company that commits to circular economy principles pressures suppliers, peers, and regulators to adopt similar practices, thereby amplifying its legacy beyond its own operations. Policy engagement extends this influence further by embedding sustainability principles into systemic frameworks that outlast individual businesses. Community and philanthropic engagement also reinforce legacy. Businesses that invest in local education, health, and infrastructure contribute to the long term prosperity of the societies in which they operate. These contributions are not peripheral but integral because they demonstrate the interdependence between business success and community wellbeing. Storytelling cements legacy by preserving narratives of challenges, breakthroughs, and impacts. Documenting and sharing sustainability journeys inspires future innovators and ensures that lessons are passed forward. Legacy is not static; it is dynamic and evolving. Companies must guard against complacency by continually seeking ways to deepen their impact and remain relevant. This involves constant innovation, ongoing research, and engagement with emerging challenges. A legacy that remains stagnant risks becoming obsolete, but a living legacy evolves with changing contexts. Global collaboration enhances legacy creation because businesses do not operate in isolation from planetary systems. Aligning strategies with international frameworks such as the United Nations Sustainable Development Goals ensures that legacies resonate beyond local markets. Participation in global networks accelerates knowledge sharing and collective progress. Ultimately the legacy of resilient and regenerative business practices represents the pinnacle of sustainable disruption. It is the moment when green innovation transcends immediate gains and becomes embedded in the long term evolution of economies and ecosystems. Such legacies are not measured only in profits but in restored landscapes, thriving communities, and enduring resilience. They ensure that future generations inherit not depletion but abundance, not fragility but resilience, not despair but hope. This is the legacy that defines true leadership in the era of sustainable disruption.